The Life of
John Bunyan

The Life of
John Bunyan

Teresa Suttles

The Christian Biography Series

ISBN-10:1530839785
ISBN-13:978-1530839780

Unless indicated otherwise, all Scripture quotations are from the King James Version 1611.

John Bunyan print from Frontispiece of *The Pilgrim's Progress* edition published in London by J. M'Gowan, 1838.

Bedford Jail print from *The Holy War* edition published in London by Cassell, Petter, and Galpin, no date.

Deed of Gift, Elstow Village, and Tomb prints from *Elstow Edition The Pilgrim's Progress* published in London by John Walker & Co., 1880

To my husband

About the Author

Teresa Suttles is a Christian educator and author. She holds graduate degrees in Christian Education and in Classical Studies.

She and her husband John, pastor of Coweta Particular Baptist Church, have four married children and nine grandchildren.

Dr. Suttles has edited a version of John Bunyan's *The Holy War* that provides a text perfect for use in families, in homeschools, and in classrooms. *The Life of John Bunyan* was the logical next step in the continued study of this renowned saint and a perfect beginning to a series of Christian biographies for the edification of the succeeding generations.

Other Books by this Author

John Bunyan's The Holy War: An Updated Version

The Little Gray Box

CONTENTS

Preface   1

Timeline   5

Introduction   9

1. A Babe and a Boy   21

2. A Soldier and a Husband   27

3. An Inquirer and a Christian   37

4. A Preacher and a Prisoner   49

5. A Saint and an Inmate   67

6. A Dreamer and an Author   83

7. A Freed Man and a Free Man   99

Epilogue   117

Endnotes   127

Bibliography   131

JOHN BUNYAN

Preface

John Bunyan has always seemed to be a near kinsman of mine – not so much because of my English ancestry, but my spiritual ancestry. Not having been reared in a Christian home, it wasn't until I was a young mother that I was introduced to Mr. Bunyan in his *The Pilgrim's Progress*. In my first reading of the book, I knew that this was my own testimony. I was Christian.

Then I met Mr. Bunyan again in his *Grace Abounding to the Chief of Sinners*, and his struggles to know Christ were my struggles to know Him. I was Bunyan.

Reading Bunyan's writings inspired me. I wanted to know the Bible as he did. When I read that very first time of Talkative – described by Faithful as chewing the cud but not dividing the hoof – I marveled at how Bunyan had ferreted out such intimate details in the Scriptures and applied them with such dexterity to my own life. This knowledge was the result of his *striving to enter in* to know Christ and then his daily struggle to walk worthy of his calling in Christ Jesus. (Luke 13:24) His testimony spurred me on and verified for me that God's Word indeed *makes wise the simple* (Psalm 19:7).

Bunyan's testimony, aligned with the heroes of the faith named in Hebrews 11, assures me again of the faithfulness of my covenant God who established me and who will strengthen me to live in obedience to Him by His precious Word. As a teacher, I encourage my students to read the Bible. Read it over and over. Learn it. Memorize it; for in the Bible are the words of life.

Many have confessed that they cannot understand the writing of Mr. Bunyan; and given the difference between the language of Bunyan's day and our own, this may be a difficulty. But let me encourage those usually too timid to venture forth into new territory that reading one of Mr. Bunyan's books will never be a waste. There is so much rich food for edification that even we modern readers can glean sufficient for our efforts. We only need to remember that Mr. Bunyan was a common, uneducated man writing for the simple folks of the villages and farms. His heart's desire and intention was to nurture them in the Word of God that they might grow in the grace and knowledge of the Lord Jesus Christ. As we read through his *The Pilgrim's Progress* or *The Holy War*, we, too, are included in that simple fellowship of believers being brought along in the faith and nurtured by the loving oversight of that tender-hearted under-shepherd of the saints.

I am blessed to have, in our personal library, several antique copies of Bunyan's various writings. One volume, printed in 1830, includes a preface written by the Reverend Samuel Wilson for an earlier edition. He wrote: "What we approve ourselves, we are apt to recommend to others." I do heartily recommend Mr. Bunyan. We can find a comradery and companionship with Bunyan as we read his allegories. He's talking about our experiences! He's describing people we know! I want to introduce you to a wonderful Christian friend in John Bunyan and to encourage you to grow your friendship with him by getting to know him in his two magnificent allegories – *The Pilgrim's Progress* and *The Holy War* – and in his inspiring autobiography *Grace Abounding to the Chief of Sinners*.

Before we begin the life of John Bunyan, we'll need to explore a bit of the history of Bunyan's day to understand why certain things happened to him; but I promise, it won't hurt a bit! Your kind patience in reading through it will reap you blessings and rewards!

Please let me thank you for reading this brief biography of my excellent friend. I wish you warm fellowship and many blessings as your own friendship with him grows!

In everybody's garden
A little rain must fall,
Or life's sweetest, fairest flowers
Wouldn't grow and bloom at all.

And though the clouds hang heavy,
So heavy Oh! my friend,
I'm sure that God who sends the shower
Will send the rainbow's end.

T.S.   (age   12)

Timeline

1603   James VI of Scotland was crowned James I of England

1611   King James Version of the Bible was commissioned

1617   Publication of the *Book of Sports*

1620   Pilgrims established Plymouth Colony in New England

1625   Charles I was crowned king

1628   Birth of John Bunyan

1630   Puritans established the Massachusetts Bay Colony in New England

1642   English Civil War began

1643   The Solemn League and Covenant

1644   John Bunyan joined New Model Army

1648   John Bunyan married Mary, his first wife

1649   King Charles I beheaded

1650   Formation of Gospel Church in Bedford with John Gifford as pastor

1658   Death of Mary Bunyan, first wife

1659   John Bunyan married Elizabeth, his second wife

1660   Charles II restored as king

1660   John Bunyan arrested first time

1661   The Corporation Act – the first of the four laws of the Clarendon Code

1662   Second Act of Uniformity

1664   Second Conventicle Act

1665   Five Mile Act

1665   Great Plague of London

1666   Published *Grace Abounding to the Chief of Sinners*

1666   Great Fire of London

1672   Declaration of Indulgence and John Bunyan released from jail

1672   Licensed as a "Congregational Person" and chosen as pastor of the Bedford Church

1675   Declaration of Indulgence recalled

1676   John Bunyan re-arrested

1677   Released from jail for the final time

1678   Published Part I of *The Pilgrim's Progress*

1682   Published *The Holy War*

1684   Published Part II of *The Pilgrim's Progress*

1685   Death of King Charles II

1688   Death of John Bunyan

1688   Glorious Revolution began

1689   Installation of William and Mary as ruling monarchs

1691   Charles Doe's publication of *The Struggler*

1691   Publication of Bunyan's *The Acceptable Sacrifice* posthumously

1691   Death of Elizabeth Bunyan, second wife

1698   Publication by Charles Doe of Bunyan's *The Heavenly Foot-man*

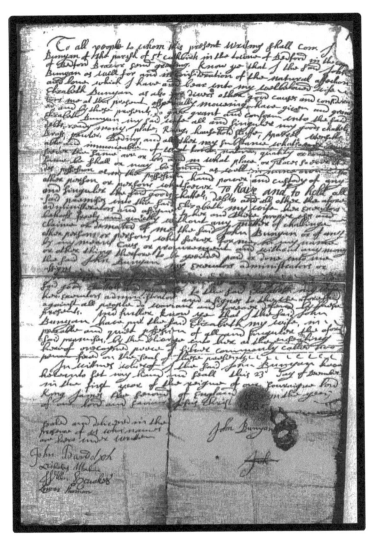

John Bunyan's Will
(Deed of Gift)

Introduction

John Bunyan was born into a specific time in history that was calling forth resolute and courageous men and women. Times were changing – drastically; and the changes were not often met with warmth and welcome from the powers who ruled. It is not absolutely necessary to explain these "winds of change" to tell the life story of Mr. Bunyan. Yet giving some brief order and explanation of the current events of his time may answer questions that often pop up in our minds and prove frustrating as we read through a book because we haven't the author at our disposal to learn the answers.

The timeline of history is punctuated by renowned figures whose abilities and courage rise above their peers. But many in every age and epoch have quietly lived and worked without the limelight of recognition, and their contributions have paved the way for that one important person who would be brought to the forefront to effect a change that would be the noteworthy contribution written about in the history books.

So at precisely the historical point of the Reformation, we will lift our timeline scroll from the shelf of Time and unroll it to the left and to the right to reveal the segment of time that shaped the life of Englishman John Bunyan of Bedford. "No great change takes place among men without suffering on the part of those who are its instruments," historian Merle D'Aubigne wrote.[1] How fitly spoken and aptly applied to our Mr. Bunyan.

The date was 31 October 1517. The German monk Martin Luther, with his *Ninety-five Theses,* had been thrust into the avant-garde of a powerful group of reformers called forth as lights in the darkness of the Middle Ages. A new day was dawning. But why was it?

With the issuance of the Edict of Milan in 313, the Roman Emperor Constantine had granted Christians the liberty to practice their religion. In the century that followed, the Christian church grew from its early New Testament founding to a more organized union of bishoprics. Theologians of great influence such as Ambrose, Chrysostom, and Augustine lived in this organizational period and were instrumental in writing the important creeds and documents that still define the tenets of Christianity today.

But the Roman Empire that had so persecuted Christians was already waning in power and influence. By 476, the Western Roman Empire had fallen to the Germanic tribes, leaving the once mighty and organized empire in disunity. A powerful alliance developed between the Germanic rulers and the bishop of Rome. This political alliance furnished the Church of Rome with the fuel necessary to organize a ruling papacy. For the next one thousand years, the nations and people were dominated by this authoritarian papal rule that claimed a divine authorization to choose or depose leaders. It was in the shrouded darkness of these long years that salvation was no longer understood by the majority of people as a *gift of God*, but as a commodity that could be earned or revoked. (Ephesians 2:8-9)

Even if the common people had had copies of the Bible, they could no longer have read it. The only translations available were in Latin, but Latin was no longer a spoken language.

The Reformation was the movement, both spiritual and political, that "emancipated not only the Church, but also the kings and people," observed D'Aubigne.[2] Luther's Germany became the flame of the movement that would reach across Europe. But long before the awakening in Germany, lights had flickered in the darkness of other places in the fallen Roman Empire.

English Christians had actually set in motion the stirrings of the Reformation long before 31 October 1517. Nine hundred years before Luther, the church of the British Isles flourished quite apart from the influence of the Roman papacy. It wasn't until the church of Britain was brought under the control of the Roman papacy that a veil of ignorance fell on the British people and shrouded the Scriptures for them. No longer did the British Christians have the Bible in their own language, even for the few people who were able to read. The British Isles came under the domination of the Roman papacy of the Middle Ages.

In 1382, the Oxford theologian and teacher John Wycliffe, with his followers the Lollards, produced a copy of the Bible in the English language. Their Bibles were illegal, and those who distributed these copies faced arrest as heretics. Wycliffe himself died before he could be arrested and condemned. But his death in 1384 did not stop the work of Scripture translation and distribution nor abate the hatred for such work. In 1415, the Council of Constance ordered that the bones of Wycliffe be dug up and burned as well as all his writings. Such a ruling made in Constance on the banks of the Rhine River was implemented in England without question. In death, Wycliffe had been condemned as a heretic; but history remembers him as the "Morning Star of the Reformation."

In 1455, Gutenberg completed the printing of the Bible on his moveable type printing press. A revolution had begun that would not be able to be controlled. This singular invention spread the flames of the Reformation. Copies of Luther's *Ninety-five Theses* and his tracts were printed and distributed throughout Europe. Once again, common people would have access to the Bible in their own language in printed copies.

The timing of Gutenberg's revolutionary invention opened the door onto the new world of exploration. Just a few years later, in 1492, Columbus would "sail the ocean blue" to find a New World where Englishmen and others could teach their children to read the Bible in their own language. But long before these hearty Englishmen left their native shores, the winds of Reformation change had begun to blow over England.

In 1509, Henry Tudor, the newly-crowned King Henry VIII of England, wed Catherine, his deceased brother's widow. Levitical law and Roman Church law forbade such a marriage, but a papal dispensation had allowed the marriage to proceed in accordance with the wishes of Henry's father. The failure of Catherine to give Henry a male heir was the impetus that finally divided Henry and his country from the papal stranglehold. Although Henry has been called the father of the English Reformation, in truth, his intentions were more out of expediency rather than religious conviction. On the contrary, his religious loyalties never changed. Henry's reformation was a power struggle with the pope. Henry wanted a divorce.

But the new printing presses had not been quiet, and Luther's writings drifted into England. Young scholars in Cambridge and Oxford read his proclamation that salvation was not by works. Many of these scholars became influential men and even martyrs in the reign of Henry VIII. William Tyndale was one of these. His English translation of the Bible was invaluable to the translators of the King James Version of 1611. In Tyndale's own lifetime, his work was not welcome – not even in Henry's England of the day.

The pope had confirmed the validity of Henry's marriage to Catherine and excommunicated Henry for divorcing her. But in 1534, Henry and his Parliament declared Henry to be "the supreme head on earth of the English Church." All the properties of the Roman Catholic Church in England would revert to Henry as this new head of the English church. Although a restructuring of clerical power followed, very little else changed in the religious life of the people. In 1536, Henry, aided by Thomas Cranmer, published the Ten Articles, outlining the doctrine of the new Established Church of England. These were followed in close succession with treatises on Christian doctrine for the common man to establish the new Anglican uniformity. But the winds of change had not blown away the old papal structures in the new state religion, and the Protestant doctrines and the English translations of the Bible were still not welcome in Henry's England. In 1536, William Tyndale was arrested on the Continent and condemned to death.

Yet the truths of the Reformation survived the successive tug-of-war between Protestant and Catholic rule after Henry's death. During the reign of Edward VI, Henry's son, Protestantism began to flourish; but disputes and fighting from controversy over the Latin mass and Protestant communion provoked the institution of the Act of Uniformity in 1549 and the required use of a Book of Common Prayer by the clergy. John Bunyan would feel the prickly fingers of this law.

With the ascension of Henry's daughter Elizabeth to the throne, many Protestant exiles returned to England. They had fled to the Continent during the rule of Henry's eldest daughter, the Catholic "Bloody Mary." Elizabeth's Act of Supremacy in 1559 was to achieve a settlement between the Protestant and Catholic factions of her domain by concluding Elizabeth to be the "Supreme Head" over all her realm in everything whether spiritual or temporal. The Act of Uniformity and the Book of Common Prayer from Edward VI's reign were restored and enforced. However, during her reign, two new versions of the English Bible were printed. Both the Bishop's Bible and the Geneva Bible had used Tyndale's New Testament. The Bishop's Bible was the Bible used in the Elizabethan churches.

The Geneva Bible had marginal notes of strong Calvinist and Puritan teaching and was the favorite of the common people.

Elizabeth's death in 1603 left no Tudor heir. James VI of Scotland, the great-grandson of Henry's sister Margaret, was crowned as James I, the first Stuart king of England. He is the king of the "King James Version" or "Authorized Version" of the English Bible, so-called because of James's authorization to produce a Bible that would be used both in the churches and by the common people.

Puritans and Independents flourished during James's reign. Their numbers and influence had grown since the days of Elizabeth, and their preaching and teaching had established a quiet observance of the Christian Sabbath, or Lord's Day, spent in study of the Bible. Rowdiness and loose living were curtailed, particularly on the Lord's Day. Ernest Bacon so aptly described the Puritans as the "most maligned and misrepresented of men"; their political enemies, particularly in the later reign of Charles II, fueled this hatred. Yet these were the men used of God, as Mr. Bacon wrote, "who brought a spiritual light to England, drew the nation back to moral values, and stamped a moral greatness upon her that no other group, religious or secular, has ever done."[3] This was the spiritual and religious climate in the days when Mr. Bunyan began to follow the Lord.

Puritan influence in the various parishes and in Parliament was beginning to rankle King James who was much in favor of sports and dancing, even on the Lord's Day. He issued his infamous *Book of*

Sports in 1617 which defined "permissible" sports that could be played on the Lord's Day as well as permission to erect May-poles and other contrivances for certain celebrations considered pagan by the Puritans. The young John Bunyan would be thrilled by such leniencies.

Although King James had attempted to restrict the Puritans, even in their sermon topics, religious life under his rule thrived for all groups. But the ascension, in 1625, of his son Charles I brought strife and civil war. Charles appointed William Laud as Archbishop of Canterbury in 1633. Laud's contempt for Puritans and their doctrine made him the perfect ally of Charles I. Together they attempted to re-institute Henry VIII's Anglican uniformity among all the groups in England and Scotland – Roman Catholics as well as Calvinist Puritans and Independents. Both Laud and Charles lost their heads in that attempt, but not before England was plunged into Civil War. Oliver Cromwell's New Model Army defeated the army of King Charles at the Battle of Naseby in 1646. King Charles became the prisoner of the Parliament until his beheading in 1649.

Parliament then abolished the use of the Book of Common Prayer and united the land under the Solemn League and Covenant. The Westminster Divines provided a directory of worship and established a Presbyterian form of church government in 1646. The young John Bunyan returned from combat duty in the New Model Army to settle down in the quiet of Cromwell's rule as Lord Protectorate. The new Commonwealth of England granted religious liberty that had not been known since the darkness of the Middle Ages had fallen over that land.

This much-loved religious liberty was quickly curtailed with the ascension of Charles II in 1660. His preference for Roman Catholicism spared him no love for the Presbyterians, Nonconformist Independents, and other dissenters of Cromwellian England. He entered into an alliance with the king of France to return England to Roman Catholicism. The rulings of Henry and Elizabeth had given him the nominal headship of the Church of England; and armed with Edward VI's Act of Uniformity and the Book of Common Prayer, he restored the episcopacy as the ruling law of the land.

These were the years of the Stuart Restoration, and the years when violators and dissidents were pursued with fervor. The Corporation Act of 1661 officially rejected the Solemn League and Covenant. The Act of Uniformity was again issued in 1662. The Conventicle Act of 1664 removed clergy who had not been ordained by the Church of England from their pulpits. With the issuance of this second Act of Uniformity and the Conventicle Act, more than two thousand Puritan ministers lost or resigned their pulpits. The Five Mile Act of 1665 forbid any minister who had not been properly ordained by the Church of England to teach in any school or to travel to within five miles of a city or town unless he vowed not to teach anything that would disagree with that Church's government or with the State. These four laws constituted the

Clarendon Code invoked to arrest and imprison Mr. Bunyan.

A Second Conventicle Act was passed by Parliament in 1670, but it was followed in 1672 by the Declaration of Indulgence. By this new leniency in the Declaration of Indulgence, Charles, always the shrewd politician, set out to honor a request to help the Quakers; but he also hoped to help his Roman Catholic friends. At the same time, he wanted to win the favor of Protestant dissenters by allowing public worship for both Protestants and Catholics. But Parliament forced the withdrawal of this declaration the next year, and in its place issued the Test Act requiring all civil and military officials to take the oath of allegiance and to take the Lord's Supper in the Church of England.

Those were dark years again for England, much as the medieval days of papal domination had been. Englishmen spied on Englishmen. Informers would follow men suspicioned of preaching without the proper license. Spies would climb trees in the dark of night to spy on barns and homes where believers may have gathered for worship. Informants infiltrated meetings. No one was safe who failed to conform to the law. Even the venerable and pious Nonconformist theologian John Owen was found by such spies and arrested. His connections and friendships from his earlier days spared him from a jail sentence. But our beloved friend John Bunyan had no such connections when he was first arrested.

At long last, the days of the Stuart Restoration ended in 1685, with the death of Charles II. It looked as though the believers would fare no better as his Catholic brother James II ascended the throne. James attempted to provide more toleration for his fellow Catholics while at the same time giving some reprieve to the dissenting Protestants by his own Declaration of Indulgence. In spite of his attempt, there was much resentment against his policy. When a son was born to James, the resentment grew into great alarm. Now this king had provided a Catholic heir to the English throne. That would not do, and James was removed from the throne and put out of the country.

Then a new and brighter day finally dawned for religious liberty in Britain. The Glorious Revolution of 1688 had removed the last vestiges of a Catholic king. Mary, the Protestant daughter of James II, and her husband William of Orange had come to the throne. In 1689, the Toleration Act was passed and many of the harsh restrictions against dissenters and Nonconformists were lifted. Persecution of these Christians was over. But it was also a time when the voice of the nation had challenged the supremacy of the monarch. The people had not wanted tolerance from a monarch. They had wanted liberty. Religious liberty – this greatest of all liberties – would transcend the globe; and all British immigrants would carry with them that same zeal that had spurred their Puritan families and neighbors to sail for the American shore. This was the dream of the Reformation.

But our dear Mr. Bunyan would only know that liberty for a brief time. His life had bracketed those most tumultuous years of British history when monarchs desperately attempted to hold on to the ancient mode of absolute rule while the roots of the Reformation liberty had taken hold. The throne of the monarch had proven no match for the Bible and the common people who believed it.

It is to the humble shire of Bedford during the years 1628 to 1688 that we'll now go, armed with the history of those times and a better understanding of Mr. Bunyan's own City of Destruction.

1

A Babe and a Boy

The dispute between Charles I and the English Puritans would doubtless not have been troubling young Thomas Bunyan and Margaret Bentley that twenty-third day in May 1627, when the record of their marriage was penned in the register of Elstow Church. Their son John later described himself as coming from a "low and inconsiderable generation" in his *Grace Abounding,* but actually the Bunyans had come from Norman stock.

Bunyan biographer Ernest Bacon in his biography *John Bunyan: Pilgrim and Dreamer* provided some historical information about Bunyan's family lineage not usually provided.[4] His name "Buignon" had originated in the Norman aristocracy and had been spelled with variations until our current spelling came to be the accepted one. According to Mr. Bacon, the early "Bonnion" ancestors in Bedfordshire had once been landowners. But through the centuries, the family had married into the peasant stock of the shire until Thomas Bunyan, Jr. was left with only two small portions of land, one of which lay in the eastern end of Elstow parish. Mr. Bacon noted that Thomas owned a large cornfield along with another field called Bunyan's Field. The Court Roll of the Manor referred to that part of the parish as "Bonyon's End."[5] The 1880 *Elstow Edition* of *The Pilgrim's Progress* verifies eleven entries in the Elstow Parish Register from 1641 to 1680 of "Bonion" and "Bunyon" family members.

Thomas Bunyan was the first of the family to describe himself as a brazier, traveling to the surrounding villages to mend kitchen knives and pots and grind scissors. Charles Doe described Thomas Bunyan as "brought up to the tinkering trade, as also were several of his brothers." Some biographers have incorrectly considered Thomas from gypsy descent. There were various groups of itinerant people who moved about the countryside and often made wooden and tin utensils to sell. From this trade, these people were given the name "tinkers." But, John S. Roberts wrote in Bunyan's biography in an 1873 edition of *The Pilgrim's Progress*:

> *Not only was John Bunyan's father not a gipsy, but he was not even a tinker such as we have described, as he dwelt in a house...The name tinker was applied to him solely on account of his being a worker in tin.*

In 1628, Thomas and Margaret welcomed their first child. The exact date of his birth is unknown, but the Elstow parish church register lists his name as John and his baptism on the 30th day of November, 1628.[6] In time, little John would be joined by his sister Margaret and brothers William and Charles. Brother Charles was born just four years before King Charles was beheaded. According to Charles Doe's biography of John Bunyan, Thomas Bunyan was "of the national religion," which may account for his son Charles's name.

Most of what can be confirmed about Bunyan's early personal life came from his own pen. But some more bits of information, including the verification of the year of his birth, were added by his friend Mr. Doe, who wrote his brief narrative on Bunyan as a preface to a folio Doe published of Mr. Bunyan's writings after the death of Bunyan. In his first paragraph of Bunyan's brief biography as recorded in *The Struggler*, Mr. Doe wrote that Bunyan was born "at Elstow, a mile side of Bedford, about the year 1628." But much of Bunyan's biography is the result of information from a very few written records such as parish registers interspersed with tradition. Vera Brittain, in her biography, articulated the dilemma of those exploring Bunyan's life as "that of deciding how far tradition and probability may be employed when direct evidence is lacking."[7]

Bunyan testified in *Grace Abounding* that in spite of the poverty of his parents "it pleased God to put it into their hearts to put me to school, to learn both to read and write..." To which school little John was sent by his parents is unknown. The *Elstow Edition* confirms that the Bedford Harpur Charity School existed at that time in Bedford and that "it is not unlikely" young Bunyan was enrolled. If this was where he was a young scholar, John would certainly have learned to read and write. By his own testimony, he retained very little of what he was taught in those school days; but whatever other subjects he may have been taught and then forgotten, he remembered those important skills of reading and writing.

John Bunyan was a boy in Elstow during the days of King James's *Book of Sports*. The biographer in the *Elstow Edition* of *The Pilgrim's Pro-*

gress described the rough crudeness of the sports and games in those days as competing "for popular favour...with the Church services on the Day of Rest." In *Grace Abounding*, Bunyan described his delight in being "taken captive by the devil at his will." He admitted that he had "few equals both for cursing, swearing, lying, and blaspheming the holy name of God"; and he became so settled in that way of life that it was like a second nature to him. John P. Gulliver wrote in his 1871 biography, "Bunyan was successful even in his wickedness." Bunyan quickly settled in as the leader of wickedness among the youth of Elstow.

As this young ringleader of profanity, Bunyan was afflicted by fearful dreams and visions. He was convinced that the Lord was so offended by his blasphemy that He plagued Bunyan with these frightening dreams of devils and wicked spirits trying to carry him off. His waking hours were often no more comforting. He was troubled by his fear of hell fire and his being there among the fiends waiting for the judgment.

Even children can experience conviction, as Bunyan himself testified. Young children, as well as adults, may be plagued from time to time with nightmares and bad dreams. But Mr. Bunyan was convinced that even as a child, his bad dreams of hell and demons came directly from the convicting work of the Holy Spirit.

By Bunyan's own testimony, these torments distressed him as a mere child of nine or ten years old. Often, he said, he was troubled even while he was playing with his friends. But distressed though he was, he could not turn away from his sins. This tug-of-war in his soul left him despairing that he would ever see heaven. If hell really existed, he reasoned that it would be better for him to be a devil himself since tormenting others would be better than being tormented. But as he tells us from his own pen in *Grace Abounding:*

> *A while after those terrible dreams did leave me, which also I soon forgot; for my pleasures did quickly cut off the remembrance of them, as if they had never been: wherefore with more greediness...I did still let loose the reins of my lusts, and delighted in all trans-gressions against the law of God: so that until I came to the state of marriage, I was the very ringleader of all the youth that kept me compa-ny, into all manner of vice and ungodli-ness...that had not a miracle of precious grace prevented, I had not only perished by the stroke of eternal justice, but had also laid myself open, even to the stroke of those laws which bring some to disgrace and open shame before the face of the world.*

Even the thoughts of religion "were very griev-ous" to Bunyan in those rebellious years, and he requested that God leave him alone. He wanted thoughts of both heaven and hell to be out of his sight and out of his mind, leaving him to live as he pleased. He wrote: "Then I said unto God, 'Depart from me, for I desire not the knowledge of thy ways.'" He ceased to care whether he was saved or lost. This new-found freedom of not caring allowed him to sin with "delight and ease."

These were the days that, in spite of Bunyan's foolish request, God did not leave him alone. God, he said, "followed me still." Yet, in spite of God's troubling Bunyan, these were not the days of Bunyan's life when God convicted him of his horrid wickedness. Rather, in those days God mixed judgment with His mercy. He spared Bunyan's life when death should have come calling. Bunyan described once falling into the creek and nearly drowning and another time falling out of a boat into the river Ouse. Both of these times, God mercifully spared his life. His boldness in folly is illustrated by the incident of his finding a venomous snake on the road. With his companion as witness, Bunyan stunned the snake with a stick, then forced open its mouth and "plucked her sting out with my fingers." But in such youthful folly, God had mercy on him.

2

A Soldier and a Husband

Mr. Bunyan himself provided very little information about his brief military career. Biographer Reverend William Brock wrote in the 1800s of Bunyan's service: "The probability is that he was a Royalist...The evidence is not conclusive; but his loyalty is so demonstrative, that he would hardly have been in arms against his sovereign."

Most early biographers disagree with Reverend Brock and the few other biographers who contended that Bunyan was a Royalist because his father was. Mr. Bacon proposed two reasons Bunyan would have joined the Parliamentary army. Bedfordshire, the county of Bunyan's home, was sympathetic to the Parliamentary army and was responsible to supply recruits for the army; and secondly, if Bunyan had fought in the Royalist army, he may not have later been imprisoned.[8]

Although early biographers disputed about whether he fought in the king's Royalist army or Parliament's New Model Army, bits of recorded information have been found that confirm Bunyan's enlistment in the New Model Army. Doubts were answered when written evidence was found in the muster rolls of the Newport Pagnell Parliamentary garrison. His mother had died when he was a young man of sixteen, just at the time recruits were being taken for this garrison at Newport Pagnell. John Bunyan is listed in the 1644 record as a private. Records indicate that he was stationed there in 1645 and again in 1647.

During these years of military service, he would have lived under the pious rules of the New Model Army. It was the intent of Cromwell and this army to have men who feared God. Independent and Nonconformist preachers would have provided constant preaching and hymn-singing; and discipline for immoral conduct and infractions of the rules was strict. These recruits would have been issued *The Souldiers Pocket Bible* with excerpts from the Geneva Bible and *The Souldiers Catechisme* written especially for the recruits of the New Model Army. During these years of soldiering, the young Bunyan probably would have been exposed continually to the preaching and teaching of the Word of God from the Puritan theological perspective. Their emphasis on personal holiness would have been a certain deterrent to Bunyan's own personal debauchery and sinfulness. The behavior of the young soldiers would have been restrained under the command of godly Puritan officers.

His testimony recounts very little about his military service. One incident from his military days he did mention when he was describing several "near-death" experiences. He linked this one "near-death" experience to God's mercifulness in saving him from death. He wrote in *Grace Abounding*:

> *This also I have taken notice of, with thanksgiving: When I was a soldier, I, with others, were drawn out to go to such a place to besiege it; but when I was just ready to go, one of*

the company desired to go in my room; to which, when I had consented, he took my place; and coming to the siege, as he stood sentinel, he was shot in the head with a musket bullet, and died.

None of these close calls were effectual to "awaken" his "soul to righteousness," as he wrote. Rather, he "sinned still, and grew more and more rebellious against God, and careless of my own salvation." In an early American Tract Society publication of *The Pilgrim's Progress*, the biographer wrote:

> *But neither mercies nor judgments made any durable impression on his hardened heart. He was not only insensible of the evil and danger of sin, but an enemy to every thing serious. The thought of religion, or the very appearance of it in others, was an intolerable burden to him.*

This was the extent of Bunyan's own record of his military service. It is doubtful he served in any major battles or that he ventured far from Newport Pagnell. But his military training and service experience provided him with knowledge for the military setting he related in *The Holy War*. He could accurately describe quartering of troops within a town and the encampment of troops about the town. No doubt, his own experience in troop reviews and parades highlighted his description of Prince Emmanuel's troops in Mansoul:

Now, when the Prince had completed these, the outward ceremonies of his joy, he again commanded that his captains and soldiers should show unto Mansoul some feats of war; so they presently addressed themselves to this work...They marched, they countermarched; they opened to the right and left; they divided and sub-divided; they closed, they wheeled, made good their front and rear with their right and left wings, and twenty things more...But add to this, the handling of their arms, and managing of their weapons of war...

Bunyan was not unfamiliar with battle strategies, whether or not he actually engaged in combat as a young soldier. In the final battle between Prince Emmanuel's army and the army of Diabolus, the Prince's army from Mansoul, when they saw Emmanuel approaching with His reinforcements, had been instructed to fall back to the walls of the town, drawing the forces of Diabolus toward them. Emmanuel's army would come up behind the enemy and trap his forces.

Then did Credence wind with his men to the townward, and gave to Diabolus the field: so Emmanuel came upon him on the one side, and the enemies' place was betwixt them both. Then again they fell to it afresh; and now it was but a little while more but Emmanuel and Captain Credence met, still trampling down the slain as they came.

Although in his own *Grace Abounding*, Bunyan did not mention any friendships from his military days, it is certain that as a soldier in the Parliamentary army, he would have heard the sermons of Puritan preachers and would have become familiar with the tenets of Puritan theology. One biographer noted that the Puritan influence was strong in the days of Bunyan's youth, and the places where he spent his childhood and military service were dominated by Puritan teaching. Many of the preachers known to Bunyan would have become influential Nonconformist ministers after the war. Later, when Bunyan himself began preaching, he may have renewed godly acquaintances with these men from his days in Newport Pagnell.

While stationed at Newport Pagnell, it is probable that Bunyan first met Matthias Cowley who may have been a bookseller in that town. Frank Mott Harrison in his biography *John Bunyan* concurs with this probability. He wrote that Matthias Cowley "within ten years of the demobilization, published the first literary venture of his conjectured comrade in arms – John Bunyan..."[9]

But when Bunyan's regiment was disbanded in 1647, he became a free man at only nineteen years of age. Troops were still garrisoned in Bedfordshire, and King Charles was a prisoner of Parliament; yet the next milestone in the life of this young, discharged soldier was marriage.

Bunyan again provided a very sparse account about his first wife. He attributed this marriage to the Providence of God, admitting that his wife came from a godly home. These young newly-weds began house-keeping in true poverty, "not having so much household stuff as a dish or spoon betwixt us both." The name of this young bride has not even been verified; but most biographers agree that it must have been Mary, since their first daughter's name was Mary. In accordance with custom, the eldest little girl was given the name of her mother. So the first wife of Bunyan is affectionately named Mary Bunyan. Her little daughter was christened in 1650, but the young parents soon learned that she was blind. Bunyan called her "my poor blind child, who lay nearer my heart than all I had beside."

This pious young wife and mother may have come into the marriage without "dish or spoon," but her contribution to the marriage was of far greater value than kitchen utensils. Her godly father had left two books to Mary that would be the extent of her wedding dowry – *The Plain Man's Pathway to Heaven*[10] and *The Practice of Piety*.[11] These books were sometimes read by Bunyan. "...I found some things that were somewhat pleasing to me," wrote Bunyan, "but all this while I met with no conviction." Mary would often tell her young husband John how her pious father had managed his household and had lived a holy life "both in word and deed."

Alas, these books were not used to work repentance in Bunyan's sad and sinful heart. They did, however, cause him to reform. As a young husband, he became a model of religion. The honesty of his confession is a sobering testimony:

...to go to church twice a day, and that too with the foremost; and there should very devoutly both say and sing, as others did, yet retaining my wicked life; but...I was so overrun with a spirit of superstition, that I adored, and that with great devotion, even all things, both the high place, priest, clerk, vestment, service, and what else belonging to the church; counting all things holy...because they were the servants, as I then thought, of God...

In those days of self-reformation, Bunyan never considered the consequences of sin. He never even thought about whether there might be a Savior. "Thus man while blind," he wrote, "doth wander, but weareth himself with vanity, for he knoweth not the way to the city of God." (Ecclesiastes 10:15)

Many are reminded from Bunyan's own testimony of the various workings of Providence in bringing them to Christ. Once, upon hearing a sermon preached on the keeping of the Sabbath, Bunyan went home convicted and depressed about his own Sabbath-breaking in playing and pleasures. But, as it turned out, his conviction was duly put to rest after a good dinner. "But oh," he wrote, "how glad was I, that this trouble was gone from me, and that the fire was put out, that I might sin again without control!" As soon as he had eaten, he "shook the sermon out of my mind, and to my old custom of sports and gaming I returned with great delight."

Yet his struggle had only begun. After his dinner on that particular Lord's Day, he had engaged with his friends in their usual afternoon games. In

the midst of his play, he was arrested with this in-
quiring thought, "Wilt thou leave thy sins and go to
heaven, or have thy sins and go to hell?" The surprise of this thought so overwhelmed him that he
stopped his play – but only momentarily. For as is
often common in the times of soul-stirring conviction, internal debate and rationalization began:

> *I had no sooner thus conceived in my
> mind, but suddenly this conclusion was fas-
> tened on my spirit...that I had been a great and
> grievous sinner, and that it was now too late
> for me to look after heaven; for Christ would
> not forgive nor pardon my transgressions.*

This very reasoning, one thought quickly following on the heels of another, brought him to despair. His conclusion was that it was too late for
him; he might as well continue in his sin. After all,
he would be miserable if he left his sins and miserable if he remained in his sins. The logical conclusion, in his mind, followed: "...I can but be
damned, and if I must be so, I had as good be
damned for many sins, as to be damned for few."

What a woeful conclusion. Bunyan resumed
his sporting with a determined resolution that his
only happiness left was what he would find in his
sin. With his own self-confirmation that heaven
was lost to him, he filled the void with his sin that
grew increasingly sweet to him. For this consuming
pursuit of sin, he laid the blame on the devil; and
looking back on his own dilemma, he concluded
that many poor sinners fall into the same trap of de-

lusion. They have concluded that there is no hope for them because "they have loved sins, 'therefore after them they will go.'" (Jeremiah 2:25)

The Village of Elstow

3

An Inquirer and a Christian

Growing into manhood in a time when the Puritans were influential in daily village lives, John Bunyan's personal assessment of his sins may have been greatly affected by the strict Puritanical assessment of personal sin. The Puritans were careful to describe their sins in the light of the Scriptures. Considering each infraction of the Law as disobedience, the Puritans applied Paul's confirmation of sin to be *that which is not of faith*. (Romans 14:23) In different times, Bunyan may not be considered to have been a gross sinner; and his youthful faults and follies would have been looked upon as the wild, recklessness of a young man.

Bunyan never confessed to having been a drunkard or immoral and promiscuous, but he did describe himself as "the very ringleader of all the youth...into all manner of vice and ungodliness." He certainly was rowdy and a notorious swearer. He was a daring risk-taker and definitely a Sabbath-breaker. His narrow escapes from drowning and death did not turn his mind to God. By his testimony, any "thoughts of religion were very grievous." He could both "sin with the greatest delight" and take pleasure in the sins of his companions. He testified that he "let loose the reins of my lusts" and "delighted in all transgressions against the law of God."

But, if Bunyan were here, he may contend that describing this list as anything less would cast him in a better light than naming them as the sins of a totally depraved and fallen sinner. He struggled with godly conviction that fueled his own attempts at self-imposed reformation. The sins which held Bunyan captive were certainly vile enough to prove indeed his very own sin nature that made him a rebel against God. He could never forget that rebellion nor cease to praise God for such grace that brought him to the Savior, and this is the theme of all he wrote. "Had not a miracle of precious grace prevented," he wrote, "I had not only perished by the stroke of eternal justice, but had also laid myself open, even to the stroke of those laws which bring some to disgrace and open shame before the face of the world." He would come to realize, with awe and thanksgiving, the grace that had protected him from injury and death in his foolish adventures and had kept him from trouble with the civil authorities.

His struggles to know Christ in the peace of personal salvation were protracted and difficult. Each crisis and each despairing doubt turned him back to searching the Scriptures. His intimate knowledge of God's Word with the appropriate application by the Lord Chief Secretary[12] was the direct result of his struggles.

By Bunyan's own testimony, he had concluded that his love for his sin had left him with no hope of salvation. Since he no longer had hope, he figured he had nothing to lose in pursuing his sin. This love of his sin had granted him the liberty to go on pursuing his sin; but as he soon found out, neither his sin nor the love of it ever seemed to bring him satisfaction. On the contrary, his notoriety as a sinner brought him shame, by his own testimony. Standing at a neighbor's shop window, he was overheard by the woman as he was cursing and swearing, which was his usual habit:

> *...one day, as I was standing at a neighbour's shop-window, and there cursing and swearing, and playing the madman, after my wonted manner, there sat, within, the woman of the house, and heard me, who, though she was a very loose and ungodly wretch, yet protested that I swore and cursed at the most fearful rate that she was made to tremble to hear me; and told me further, that I was the ungodliest fellow for swearing, that she ever heard in all her life; and that I, by thus doing, was able to spoil all the youth in the whole town...*
>
> *At this reproof I was silenced, and put to secret shame; and that too, as I thought, before the God of heaven...But how it came to pass I know not; I did from this time forward so leave my swearing, that it was a great wonder to myself to observe it...All this while I knew not Jesus Christ, neither did I leave my sports and plays.*

As is often the case in the lives of troubled sinners, Bunyan began to keep company with a poor man who called himself a Christian. Their talks about the Bible and religion prompted Bunyan to begin reading his own Bible. He especially liked the historical parts; but as he said, he couldn't understand Paul's letters "and suchlike Scriptures."

This reading of the Bible led him into an outward reformation of his life. He wanted to keep the Ten Commandments as his way of getting to heaven. He was successful at times, he thought; but then he would fail. This would be followed by a repenting and promising God "to do better next time."

In his reforming days, Bunyan was convinced that he "pleased God as well as any man in England." Even his neighbors were convinced that his reformed behavior was the proof of his new religious life as they discussed his amazing conversion from a cursing rebel. Their praise only served to puff him up with pride; for he wrote, "...it pleased me mighty well." He knew he was only a "poor painted hypocrite," but he "loved to be talked of as one that was truly godly." All of his actions sprang from his one motive to be admired. He was proud of his outward godliness and ordered his behavior that he might "be well spoken of by man." "But," as one biographer wrote, "all this was only lopping off the branches of sin, while the root of an unregenerated nature still remained."[13]

During these days of his self-reforming hypocrisy, he was participating in the ringing of the bells in the church belfry. According to tradition, Bunyan lustily rang bell Number Four at practices and also for each Lord's Day. Interestingly, he began to be uneasy about participating in the activity that was a cause for such personal vanity. He reckoned such vanity was really not proper for a religious man and gave up his beloved bell-ringing. Although he resigned his position, he would stand in the belfry watching the ringers. Then he became plagued by the thoughts that one of the bells may fall. He relocated himself to watch, standing under a main, supporting beam across the steeple. Still, he reckoned that a bell could come unfastened in a swing, hit the wall, and rebound on him, killing him anyway. He moved again to stand in the doorway where he figured he would be safe. "If a bell should then fall," he had reasoned, "I can slip out behind these thick walls, and so be preserved." But the peace of this safe place did not last long. He began to think that the whole steeple could fall; and he became so afraid, that he no longer even stood in the steeple doorway.

His continued love of these bells in his later years is seen in the verses of his *The Pilgrim's Progress* when the bells of the Celestial City rang to welcome Christian and Hopeful:

> *Here also they had the city itself in view; and they thought they heard all the bells therein to ring, to welcome them thereto.*

In his *A Book for Boys and Girls* published in 1686, he wrote poem XXIX about bells:

> *When Ringers handle them with Art and Skill, They then the ears of their Observers fill, With such brave Notes, they ting and tang so well As to outstrip all with their ding, dong, Bell.*
>
> *O Lord! If Thy poor Child might have his will And might his meaning freely to Thee tell,*

He never of this Musick has his fill,
There's nothing to him like thy ding, dong, Bell.

John Bunyan was like so many before him and so many who have followed. He could not find the *peace that passeth all understanding* in all his own reformation. (Philippians 4:7) He described himself as a "poor wretch" who was still ignorant of Jesus Christ, yet busily attempting to establish his own righteousness. He certainly would have perished he wrote, "...had not God in mercy showed me more of my state by nature."

In all of God's mercies to Bunyan, there was that one certain day that forever was pressed into his memory. He had gone into the village of Bedford for his work and happened to pass the place where three or four women sat in a doorway talking about the things of God. His confidence as a "brisk talker also myself in the matters of religion" gave him boldness to draw close to hear their conversation. But sadly for him, "they were far above, out of my reach." They were talking about the new birth and how God had worked in their sinful hearts. As he described their conversation: "Their talk was about a new birth, the work of God on their hearts...They talked how God had visited their souls with His love in the Lord Jesus..."

Their discussion of God's deliverance for them from their particular temptations of Satan was of special interest to him since his own soul had been so afflicted by these same torments. But what puzzled Bunyan was the pleasure they had in speaking about the Bible as if they had found a new world and no longer lived among their neighbors.

Yet the wonder of their conversation left Bunyan trembling with the astonishing realization that he had never once thought about this new birth. He had never known such comfort, nor had he understood the deceitfulness of his own heart and the temptations of Satan. He was convinced by their conversation that he, in spite of all his reforming behavior, lacked "the true tokens of a truly godly man." At last, he saw that only the "truly godly" were happy and blessed.

Bunyan returned again and again to listen to the conversation of these good women. Two things began to happen from these visits. He was overcome with a "very great softness and tenderness of heart," as he described it, which brought him under conviction and convinced him that what they told him from the Bible was true. He also experienced "a great bending in my mind" that spurred him to a continual meditation of the Scriptures. He even found that he kept remembering all the other good things he had previously heard and read.

Now the Bible became precious to him. The letters of the apostle Paul, which once had been too hard for him to understand, were now sweet to him. He described himself in those days as always being in the Bible – either reading it or thinking about it. Yet, even in those days of searching the Scriptures, he wrestled with doubts about his faith and with the distress that God would not show him mercy unto salvation. He lamented the years he had spent in sin when he had "no more wit, but to trifle away my time till my soul and heaven were lost." But as soon as the good women of Bedford learned of his distress, they talked to their pastor; and he came to visit Bunyan.

Pastor John Gifford had been a major in the Royalist army and had been taken prisoner in the Civil War. The night before his execution, he had escaped to London. Later, he settled in Bedford in the practice of medicine. He became a notorious sinner in the town, known for his violent hatred of the Puritans. According to the providential working of God, he was brought to a deep conviction of his own sinfulness after reading Robert Bolton's *The Four Last Things: Death, Judgement, Hell, and Heaven.* Gifford's conversion was openly testified in his changed life and fellowship with the Puritans of Bedford he had once reviled. At the time he met John Bunyan about 1651, he was the minister of the Independent congregation then meeting in the St. John's Church building in Bedford which had been vacated by the Episcopal minister during the time of Cromwell's Protectorate.

Mr. Gifford visited Bunyan and invited Bunyan to visit in his home and in the church meetings. Although Bunyan spent time in Mr. Gifford's home and attended the services at the church, he spent several months in affliction and wrestlings of his soul. During this time of personal anguish, Bunyan wrote of two things that made him wonder, particularly as he considered the lives of professing Christians. "The one was," he said, "when I saw old people hunting after the things of this life, as if they should live here always." And in his particular consideration of Christians, he wrote, "…when I found professors much distressed and cast down when they met with outward losses; as of husband, wife, child, etc." His thoughts were all in turmoil about his eternal soul, without regard for things of this world. He wrote: "Were my soul but in a good condition, and were I but sure of it, ah! how rich should I esteem myself, though blessed but with bread and water! I should count those but small afflictions, and should bear them as little burthens. 'But a wounded spirit, who can bear?'"[14] (Proverbs 18:14) Little did he know in those days of anguish, that these "small afflictions" would also be his to bear later in his Christian life.

It was during this time of conviction and searching that a copy of Martin Luther's *Commentary on Galatians* came into Bunyan's possession. He had longed to learn about the experience of a godly man from ancient days because he was convinced that those godly men who were living in his day only wrote about the experiences of others.

> *…I did greatly long to see some ancient godly man's experience, who had writ some hundreds of years before I was born; for those who had writ in our days, I thought (but I desire them now to pardon me) that they had writ only what others felt…without going down themselves into the deep.*

By the time Bunyan penned his own autobiography, he wisely begged the pardon for the youthful error of his own ignorance in such spiritual matters as his measuring the experiences of different Christians. But the graciousness of the Lord was certainly manifested on this earnest seeker with the granting of this desire. "After many such longings in my mind, the God in whose hands are all our days and ways did cast into my hand...a book." When Bunyan had read just a little from this tattered copy, he found that Luther was addressing Bunyan's own particular afflictions. Luther discussed temptations and the Law as well as Satan, death, and hell. This book, except for the Bible, gave more comfort to Bunyan than anything else had been able to do. He called it the "most fit for a wounded conscience." But he testified again and again that it was the words of Scripture that most salved and assured his afflicted soul. These times of desperate searching in the Bible for the words of life applied personally to him gave Bunyan such tender familiarity with the Holy Scriptures that he could suck the most delicate nuances forth from the obscurest of passages so often over-read by those of less tormented consciences. "The Scriptures now also were wonderful things unto me. I saw that the truth and verity of them were the keys of the kingdom of heaven," he wrote of those days.

At long last, the comfort came he had so longed desired. The words came into his heart, "I must go to Jesus." It was at that moment the "former darkness and atheism fled away, and the blessed things of heaven were set within my view." Then he remembered the phrase from Hebrews 12:22: *and to an innumerable company of angels.* "That night was a good night to me, I never had but few better," he wrote. "Christ was a precious Christ to my soul that night; I could scarce lie in my bed for joy, and peace, and triumph, through Christ." Referring to the words of Hebrews 12:22-24, he wrote, "These words also have oft since this time, been great refreshment to my spirit. Blessed be God for having mercy on me!" These words he recorded again in his *The Pilgrim's Progress* as Christian and Hopeful went up the hill to the holy city:

> *The talk that they had with the shining ones was about the glory of the place; who told them, that the beauty and glory of it was inexpressible. There, said they, is "Mount Zion, the heavenly Jerusalem, the innumerable company of angels, and the spirits of just men made perfect."*

Based on his earliest biographer Charles Doe, it remains the consensus of Bunyan's later biographers that he was admitted to the Independent Church meeting in St. John's Church building in Bedford where John Gifford was the pastor about the year 1653. Doe dates Bunyan's baptism between the years 1651 and 1653 in a small creek feeding into the river Ouse at the end of Duck Lane in Bedford. Disagreements arise among the biographers as to whether or not Bunyan was baptized as Doe claimed or was simply admitted to the fellowship of believers. Others boldly assert that the congregation was a Baptist congregation, while others adamantly deny such claims. But the conclusion of his two arduous years of personal conviction and of struggle to know the comfort and peace through Christ is sweetly summed up in the tender words of the biographer writing for an old American Tract Society publication: "When twenty-seven years of age, Mr. Bunyan joined a congregation of pious Christians at Bedford."

4

A Preacher and a Prisoner

John and Mary Bunyan were blessed with the arrival of baby Elizabeth in 1654. In the year following Elizabeth's birth, the Bunyans moved from the village of Elstow to a cottage in Bedford to be nearer the congregation meeting in the St. John's Church building and pastored by the beloved John Gifford.

Frank Mott Harrison, a Bunyan biographer, included this description of the Nonconformist congregation in Bedford: "'In the year 1650, Mr. Gifford, and eleven serious Christians appointed a day when they should meet, and, after fervent prayer, they dedicated themselves to God. This done, the eleven chose Gifford as their pastor...'"[15] Since that day of prayer and dedication, the tiny congregation had grown in membership; and many people from the surrounding villages regularly attended the meetings led by Mr. Gifford. John Bunyan's name was added to the list of faithful members; and like the others, he was to *grow in the grace and knowledge of the Lord Jesus Christ* under the faithful ministry of Pastor Gifford. (II Peter 3:18) But the earthly ministry of pious Mr. Gifford would be concluded in September 1655.

Bunyan gathered with other members of Gifford's flock around his bedside as the pastor dictated his last words to the saints of Bedford. The dictation of his instructions and admonitions being signed by his own hand, the pastor crossed over to the Celestial City. The young Mr. Bunyan would later honor his dear pastor in "the picture of a very grave person" hanging on the wall in a private room of Interpreter's house with the following description in *The Pilgrim's Progress*:

It had eyes lifted up to heaven, the best of books in its hand, the law of truth was written upon its lips, the world was behind its back. It stood as if it pleaded with men, and a crown of gold did hang over its head.

At Christian's inquiry, Interpreter explained:

The man whose picture this is, is one of a thousand; he can beget children, travail in birth with children, and nurse them himself when they are born. And, whereas thou seest him with his eyes lifted up to heaven, the best of books in his hand, and the law of truth writ on his lips; it is to show thee, that his work is to know and unfold dark things to sinners; even as also thou seest him stand as if he pleaded with men; and, whereas thou seest the world as cast behind him, and that a crown hangs over his head, that is to show thee, that slighting and despising the things that are present for the love that he hath to his Master's service, he is sure, in the world that comes next, to have glory for his reward.

In January 1656, the congregation at Bedford called John Burton as pastor. John and Mary Bunyan, by that time, had a third young child. This son was also named John and would serve the Lord during his lifetime as a member of that Bedford congregation. It is possible that Bunyan served as deacon in the congregation; but church records, commencing in May 1656, indicate that Bunyan began public preaching sometime in that same year.[16]

Mr. Bunyan wrote in his *Grace Abounding* that "after I had been about five or six years awakened, and helped myself to see both the want and worth of Jesus Christ our Lord," some of the saints among the Bedford congregation recognized that God had given Bunyan an understanding of the Word and "utterance in some measure, to express what I saw to others for edification." Bunyan described these friends as "saints...the most able for judgment and holiness of life." At their urging, he finally consented to speak at small gatherings; but soon, he accepted invitations to travel into the countryside around Bedford to speak in a more public forum. He was formally appointed to the public preaching of the Word by the members of the Bedford Church.

Biographer Frank Mott Harrison explained that these Bedford Christians recognized that Bunyan was "no ordinary convert" and that Bunyan had "unwittingly given evidence" of his gifts of preaching and teaching.[17] Bunyan, unlike so many of the godly Puritan preachers of his day, had no formal schooling or theological training. But as Mr. Mott observed, Bunyan's soul-searching experiences to know Christ had "done more to equip him...than any academic training could do." This lack of formal, theological training was no deterrent to the saints in Bedford who ordained Mr. Bunyan, as he wrote himself, "to a more ordinary and public preaching of the Word, not only to and amongst them that believed, but also...to those who had not yet received the faith." This ordination was accompanied by the desire to preach to the unsaved, not, as Bunyan confessed, for the desire of glorifying himself since he was at that very time being "afflicted with the fiery darts of the devil, concerning my eternal state."

But those fiery darts could not restrain Mr. Bunyan. Jeremiah's testimony became Mr. Bunyan's own. Jeremiah testified that ...*his word was in mine heart as a burning fire shut up in my bones*...(Jeremiah 20:9). Bunyan wrote that he could not "be content" unless he was exercising this gift of exhortation and preaching. His own burning desire to minister to the saints was coupled with his conviction of Paul's admonition in I Corinthians 16:15-16 that the gifts of the Holy Spirit were not to be buried but to be exercised in the work of the ministry. ...*they have addicted themselves to the ministry of the saints* (I Corinthians 16:15).

As Bunyan exercised his calling to the ministry of the saints and to the preaching of the Gospel, he recorded that people "came in to hear the Word by hundreds, and that from all parts." God filled him with pity for the souls of these people, and his concern was evident in his preaching. Many came to Christ, and he wrote how this caused him great rejoicing. "Yea," Bunyan wrote, "the tears of those whom God did awaken by my preaching would be both solace and encouragement to me." He never forgot the difficult way of his own salvation. He described the early days of his ministry:

> *Indeed I have been as one sent to them from the dead. I went myself in chains, to preach to them in chains, and carried that fire in my own conscience that I persuaded them to beware of.*

His message was "to hold forth Jesus Christ in all His offices, relationships, and benefits unto the world..." His heart's desire in all his preaching, he wrote, was that God would "make the Word effectual to the salvation of the soul..." This was the major context of all his preaching, particularly in those early years of ministry. He believed that he must preach with full earnestness and commitment the "word of faith, and the remission of sin by the death and sufferings of Jesus," as he explained. This message alone consumed his ministry; and all other things, he left alone. He made no attempt to meddle in the controversies among Christians since these controversies, as he had observed, only brought strife. "My work," he wrote, "did run in another channel, even to carry an awakening word; to that therefore I did stick and adhere."

Interestingly, Bunyan's sermons were fresh and completely exclusive. He preferred to refrain from using other men's thoughts and sermon references. He appropriated the words of Paul in Galatians 1:11-12 as his own testimony: *But I certify you, brethren, that the gospel which was preached of me is not after man. For I neither received it of man, neither was I taught it, but by the revelation of Jesus Christ.* His own personal struggle and search to know the peace and assurance of his salvation had indeed opened up to him the very nuances of Scripture and had provided him with what he believed the only basis of confirmation as he preached the Word of God to others. He described his sermons in *Grace Abounding*: "...I verily thought, and found by experience, that what was taught me by the Word and Spirit of Christ, could be spoken, maintained, and stood to by the soundest and best established conscience..."

Certainly there was no surprise that when Bunyan began to travel out from Bedford to preach, the preachers in those other places were against him. Fallacious rumors spread abroad from the lips of his accusers. These rumors ran the gamut from accusing him of being a witch to being a highwayman. The most contrary and reprehensible of all the accusations were those slanderous accusations of adulteries. To these particular charges, Bunyan made specific answer in his last revision of *Grace Abounding*:

These things therefore, upon my own account, trouble me not; no, though they were twenty times more than they are. I have a good conscience; and whereas they speak evil of me, as an evil-doer, they shall be ashamed that falsely accuse my good conversation in Christ...

Therefore, I bind these lies and slanders to me as an ornament. It belongs to my Christian

*profession to be vilified, slandered, re-
proached, and reviled...*

Mr. Bunyan actually gloried in these slanders
he described as the work of the devil against him.
He concluded that if he were not treated with such
wickedness by the world, he would require a sign
that he was actually a saint or a child of God. Rather than dwell upon such matters he was consumed
with Christ and with bringing sinners to Him. He
wrote of his ministry: "...I did often say in my
heart before the Lord, that if to be hanged up presently before their eyes, would be a means to awaken
them, and confirm them in the truth, I gladly should
be contented."

But the slanderous rumors did have their effect.
Bunyan recognized that "Satan labored by re-
proaches and slanders to make me vile among my
countrymen..." Those who promoted such rubbish
were instruments to render Bunyan's preaching in-
effective; but another sad result was, as he understood himself, to add to his "long and tedious imprisonment..." which they hoped would frighten
Bunyan from his service for Christ and to make the
world afraid to hear him preach.

Even though Bunyan had begun preaching during the time of Cromwell's Protectorate, hostilities
still flared among some who resented such an itinerant preacher preaching in the pulpits of ordained
ministers. One such incident was a shadowy por-
tent of future ill winds for Bunyan. In December
1657, he preached in the parish of Eaton. The Reverend Thomas Becke had been appointed to the par-

ish church by the House of Lords and was a foe of
the Independents.[18] His belief in a well-educated
ministry fueled his hostility against the uneducated
tinker coming to preach in his parish. Becke was
able to secure an indictment against Bunyan that
was to be heard at the following Bedford assizes.[19]
The Bedford congregation was called to a day of
prayers for Bunyan; and although no apparent consequences came from the indictment, Bunyan realized the risk of preaching in the pulpits of ordained
clergy.

This was but the leading cloud of that edge of
dark clouds of trial and testing that would move into
Bunyan's life. In 1658, Mary Bunyan gave birth to
their fourth child, a son named Thomas. She never
seemed to regain her strength; and sometime in that
same year Mary died, leaving Bunyan, not yet thirty, with four young children. Following the prayer-
ful counsel of the Bedford congregation, John married his second wife Elizabeth sometime in 1659.
Nothing more is known of Elizabeth prior to their
marriage; but from Bunyan's own testimony, she
was a loving helpmeet and godly mother to his children.

In the years after his conversion, Bunyan had
again come into contact with William Dell who had
served as a chaplain in the Parliamentary army.
Dell had been educated in Cambridge during the
flourishing times of Puritanism and had, in the years
following the Civil War, served in various ecclesi-
astical capacities. In December 1659, Dell, the
Rector of Yelden Church, invited Bunyan to preach
at Yelden. At the family meal following the ser-

vice, John Bunyan met Dell's daughter Mercy, who probably served as the model in later years for Mercy in *The Pilgrim's Progress*. But the after-dinner discussions of these two godly men focused on the precarious state of affairs in their country. Cromwell had died in September 1658, and the government had become unsteady under the rule of his son Richard. The scholarly Dell, being the elder of the two men, predicted a return of the monarchy and an end to the religious liberties of the Puritans that had been afforded under the Protectorate.

Six months later, in June 1660, Dell's disgruntled parishioners sent a petition to the House of Lords lodging complaints against their Nonconformist vicar. Their complaints listed his neglect of the sacraments and also his allowance of the uneducated tinker John Bunyan to speak in the pulpit of the congregation. This first petition of grievance against Dell was dismissed by the House of Lords; but just as his friend Bunyan had experienced the earnest of such treatment to come, Dell himself was ejected from his pulpit in 1662 with the Act of Uniformity.

It may well be said by some that 1660 was the *annus horribilis* (horrible year) for the Puritans and Nonconformists left adrift by the death of Oliver Cromwell. The anarchy that had ensued culminated in the restoration of the monarchy as William Dell had predicted. In May 1660, Charles II was greeted with the presentation of an English Bible by the Mayor of Dover. Before 1660 concluded, the episcopacy had been restored and many Independent and Puritan ministers had been removed from their pulpits and their livings. Many also lost their positions as teachers since Puritans were no longer welcome in the universities.

The Independent congregation in Bedford suffered double grief when they lost both their beloved pastor John Burton and their meeting place in August of that difficult year of 1660. Bunyan had been called upon to fill the pulpit during Burton's months of illness, but now the church was faced with the death of Burton and the calling of a new pastor. Their heartaches were compounded when the aged Episcopal clergyman Theodore Crowley was restored to his pulpit, and the Established Church services resumed at St. John's Church. The faithful group, organized and growing under the leadership of their late pastors John Gifford and then John Burton, was left without a pastor and a meeting place. The times of testing had begun in earnest.

Edward Hyde, Lord Clarendon, began the restoration of the prelacy. The Episcopal Church was to be restored as it had been prior to the Civil War, and this was to be accomplished by the institution of the Clarendon Code. The Second Act of Uniformity was not passed until 1662, but it was already casting its long shadow late in that year 1660. Independents and Nonconformists all over England, including the Bedford congregation, had to search for meeting places in private residences and later in barns and cowsheds.

John Bunyan's name had previously aroused attention with Becke's indictment in 1657. Already being a published author, Bunyan's renown as a prominent Nonconformist preacher had grown; and with it, the issuance of a warrant for his arrest by the local magistrate Mr. Francis Wingate. Elizabeth Bunyan was expecting her first child in that December 1660. It was on the 12th of that November that John Bunyan left his young wife and four little children to attend a preaching engagement some thirteen miles from Bedford. The meeting was to be held in a farmhouse at Lower Samsell near Harlington in the county of Bedford. Bunyan was well-known in that area, having often preached there.

When he entered the room, those attending were anxious and fearful. They had learned of Wingate's warrant. Some were certain the house was being watched. Bunyan was urged to forego preaching and make his escape. He walked alone out into a field to prayerfully consider this crisis that had been so clearly foreseen.

John Bunyan refused to flee. He reckoned that any attempt of escape would shake the faith of the believers that such a preacher had been stronger in his words than in his deeds, and it would also give the enemies of God a reason to blaspheme. He wrote in his own autobiographical account *A Relation of the Imprisonment of Mr. John Bunyan*:

> *Also I feared that if I should run now there was a warrant out for me, I might by so doing make them afraid to stand when great words only should be spoken to them.*
> *Besides, I thought that seeing God of his mercy should choose me to go upon the forlorn hope in this country – that is, to be the first that should be opposed for the Gospel – if I should*

fly it might be a discouragement to the whole body that might follow after.[20]

What a designation that Bunyan should have seen himself as the "forlorn hope," the first of many who would suffer for the sake of the Gospel in that forlornness then resurrected in his own country of England.

He opened the meeting with prayer. Before he had spoken more than a few sentences on his chosen text, the constable and a servant entered the room, brandishing the warrant for his arrest. Bunyan was seized to be led out of the meeting. But he was able to speak a few parting words of encouragement to those who had gathered to hear the preaching of the Word. He reminded them that they had all gathered to hear the Word of God; and in days to come, they were likely to suffer for that very action. But he encouraged them to consider that it was a mercy to suffer for such a reason:

> *...for we might have been apprehended as thieves or murderers, or for other wickedness; but, blessed be God! it was not so, but we suffer as Christians for well-doing, and we had better be the persecuted than the persecutors...*

Bunyan was led across the fields to the house of Francis Wingate about a mile away in Harlington. Mr. Wingate was away for the night, but a neighboring farmer made himself surety and lodged Bunyan for the night. The next morning, Bunyan was taken before the magistrate Francis Wingate in Harlington House.

Wingate was a country gentleman whose jurisdiction as a justice of the peace and country magistrate was limited in that area. Many Nonconformists would soon take advantage of Wingate's limited jurisdiction and hold meetings close to county borders to allow for easy escape into a neighboring county. Bunyan would refer to this in his description of the escape of Christian and Hopeful from Giant Despair in *The Pilgrim's Progress*:

> *But that gate as it opened made such a creaking that it waked Giant Despair, who hastily rising to pursue his prisoners, felt his limbs to fail, for his fits took him again, so that he could by no means go after them. Then they went on, and came to the King's highway again, and so were safe, because they were out of his jurisdiction.*

John Bunyan, the prisoner, was brought by the constable before Francis Wingate. The constable was questioned about the meeting and whether he had seen the presence of weapons. None had been seen, and only a few persons had gathered to hear the preaching of the Word. Having found no grave offenses thus far, Mr. Wingate began to question Bunyan himself. At long last, these two men of about the same age faced each other.

Wingate wanted to know what Bunyan was doing at this meeting. Bunyan calmly replied that he had come to instruct and counsel the people to follow Christ. Wingate, unabashed, asked if Bunyan was aware that it was against the law for him to do so. Why could Bunyan not be content to follow his trade? Again, Bunyan calmly replied that he could both follow his trade and preach the Word. This stoked the ire of Mr. Wingate, who duly threatened to "break the neck" of those meetings.

Francis Wingate then demanded sureties for Bunyan that would guarantee his appearance before the next assizes. His threatening to put Bunyan in prison brought forward some of Bunyan's friends to act as sureties. As Wingate had the bond drawn up, he warned the guarantors that if Bunyan preached again before the Quarter Sessions, they would forfeit their bond. At this threat, Bunyan intervened, releasing his friends from their bonds. He told Wingate plainly that he would not refrain from speaking the Word of God. "And," he said to Wingate, "I thought this to be a work that had no hurt in it, but was rather worthy of commendation than blame." Wingate then left the room to write the court order committing John Bunyan to the Bedford Gaol (jail).

In the interval, the vicar Dr. William Lindall (Bunyan called him Dr. Lindale) entered the room. Bunyan referred to him as an "old enemy to the truth" who had come in to taunt Bunyan "with many reviling terms." Lindall charged Bunyan with meddling and asked if he had taken the oaths; and if he had not, it was a pity since Bunyan would be sent to prison. He sparred with Bunyan briefly concerning the Scriptures; but Bunyan remembered the Scriptural admonition to "*Answer not a fool accord-*

ing to his folly," and so was "as sparing of my speech as I could without prejudice to the truth." (Proverbs 26:4)

The mittimus, or court order, having been prepared by Wingate and handed to the constable, Bunyan was escorted from the house. Two of Bunyan's friends intervened, asking the constable to give them time to speak with the magistrate on Bunyan's behalf. So Bunyan was again escorted into the house, but he was never convinced that he would be released unless he was willing to dishonor God. He lifted up his soul in prayer that God may give him light and strength to be kept from doing anything that would dishonor Him, or wrong his own soul, or be a discouragement to anyone who may be seeking to know the Lord Jesus Christ.

By this time, the evening darkness had fallen; and Bunyan was seen by Dr. William Foster of Bedford, Wingate's brother-in-law and a champion of the episcopacy. Foster showed such seeming affection toward Bunyan that Bunyan was made to wonder why such a man as Foster would show so much love to such a man as himself. But as they conversed, Bunyan remembered the words: *Their tongues are smoother than oil, but their words are drawn swords* (Psalm 55:21).

Foster attempted to dissuade Bunyan from calling people together and to simply follow his calling as a brazier. He assured Bunyan that Wingate was loath to send him to jail. But Bunyan protested that he had not compelled any one to come to hear him preach; yet, if they came together, he would certainly exhort them to seek the Lord Jesus Christ. Then

Foster kindly reminded him that such meetings were against the law and that Bunyan must leave off preaching and follow his calling. Bunyan assured Foster that he believed it his duty to do the most good he could both in his trade and in communicating to all people the best understanding he had of God's Word. Foster claimed Bunyan was ignorant of the Scriptures since he did not know the original Greek and that only the foolish people listened to him. Bunyan reminded him of the Scripture, "that God hides his things from the wise and prudent, (that is, from the learned of the world) and reveals them to babes and sucklings." (Matthew 11:25) Foster simply reminded him again that if he would promise not to call the people together, he could be free to go home.

After Foster left the room, servants of Wingate entered with the message that Wingate was willing to grant him his liberty if only he would promise not to call the people together. Bunyan answered that there were more ways than one that a man could be accused of calling people together. For instance, a man might simply read a book in the market-place; and in so doing, a crowd of people gather around him. This might be termed a calling of the people together. So then by the same argument, Bunyan explained, his own preaching may be said to call people together. Dr. Foster then, who had, at first, shown so much love toward Bunyan, told Wingate that Bunyan must be sent to prison.

Bunyan wrote that he wanted to testify to all gathered there of the peace that God had given him, but he refrained from speaking. Rather, he said that he blessed the Lord and went away to prison, "with God's comfort in my poor soul."

The Bedford Jail

5

A Saint and an Inmate

The Psalmist said that the Lord would teach each of His saints in the way that He would choose (Psalm 25:12), and so it was with John Bunyan. His constancy to the Word and calling of God had placed him at the head of the line of those who would feel the pinch of the ascendency of Charles II and Lord Clarendon, his implacable, unrelenting advocate for the exclusiveness of the episcopacy.

Dear Bunyan's lack of "letters" and ignorance of the politics that put men into the recognized pulpits would not prevent him from holding tenaciously to his calling and his responsibility to exercise it. He believed as had Peter, that he *ought to obey God rather than men* (Acts 5:29). For this integrity and determination to hold truth, Bunyan would learn the meaning of the words of Revelation 14:12: *Here is the patience of the saints: here are they that keep the commandments of God, and the faith of Jesus.*

The news of John Bunyan's arrest spread among the members of the Bedford congregation. "After I had lain in the jail five or six days," Bunyan wrote, "the brethren sought means to get me out by bondsmen…" These were the terms of Wingate's order. Bunyan was to remain in jail until some person or persons would stand as surety that Bunyan would appear at the upcoming Quarter Sessions of the Bedford assizes. These church friends of Bunyan petitioned Mr. Crumpton, the magistrate at Elstow, to accept bond for Bunyan.

But Mr. Crumpton requested to read the actual mittimus written by Wingate which read in part, as Bunyan later wrote, "That I went about to several conventicles in this country, to the great disparagement of the government of the Church of England..." Upon reading Wingate's description of the charges, Crumpton decided that there could be something more against Bunyan than was named in the mittimus. Bunyan described Crumpton as a young man and considered that this may be the reason he refused to issue the bond.

Yet Bunyan was undaunted. He regarded Crumpton's response as evidence that the Lord had heard his prayer. He wrote in *A Relation of the Imprisonment of Mr. John Bunyan:*

> *For before I went down to the justice, I begged of God that if I might do more good by being at liberty than in prison, that then I might be set at liberty, but if not, His will be done; for I was not altogether without hopes but that my imprisonment might be an awakening to the saints in the country; therefore I could not tell well which to choose, only I, in that manner, did commit the thing to God.*

The sweet spirit with which Bunyan resigned himself to the will of God is summed up in his closing remark about the specifics of his arrest: "And verily at my return I did meet my God sweetly in the prison again, comforting of me and satisfying of me that it was His will and mind that I should be there."

Regarding his imprisonment and musing on the response of the magistrate, he wrote:

> *Let the rage and malice of men be never so great, they can do no more nor go no farther than God permits them; but when they have done their worst, "We know that all things work together for good to them that love God."*

John Bunyan's arrest occurred less than six months after Charles II assumed the throne. The various laws of the Clarendon Code had not yet been installed, but the intent was already enforced. Sadly, Bunyan was arrested for breaking Elizabethan laws still remaining on the statue books. One such law required church attendance in the Established Church every Sunday and holy day or face public censure and fines. A second law invoked for his arrest made it illegal and punishable by imprisonment to attend religious meetings known as conventicles. Banishment followed for those who refused obedience to these laws.

Seven weeks passed, and Bunyan remained in the jail until the next Quarter Sessions were held in Bedford in January 1661. He recounted, with clarity of memory, his presentation by his jailer to the justices of the assizes. His recollection is in the form of a narrative and exactly resembles his choice of presentation in the trial proceedings by Mansoul on behalf of the Prince against the Diabolonians arrested in Mansoul in *The Holy War.*

"There was a bill of indictment preferred against me," he wrote in his account of his imprisonment. His recitation of the indictment reads:

> *That John Bunyan, of the town of Bedford, labourer, being a person of such and such conditions, he hath, since such a time, devilishly and perniciously abstained from coming to church to hear Divine service, and is a common upholder of several unlawful meetings and conventicles, to the great disturbance and distraction of the good subjects of this kingdom, contrary to the laws of our sovereign lord the king, etc.*

The clerk of the court responded to the reading of the indictment by asking Mr. Bunyan for his reply to the indictment. Bunyan replied that he was "a common frequenter of the Church of God, and was also, by grace, a member with those people over whom Christ is the Head."

Justice Sir John Kelynge inquired if Bunyan attended church, verifying that he meant the parish church.[21] Bunyan replied that he did not; and when asked the reason, he replied that he did not find it commanded in the Word of God. Kelynge responded that they were commanded to pray, but Bunyan verified that the commandment was not restricted to the Common Prayer Book.

An interrogation then ensued with other of the justices interjecting questions on the use of the prayer book to regulate proper prayers. Bunyan's responses were always couched in Scripture. At last, he was asked directly why he was so against the Common Prayer Book. He asked permission to give his reasons; and such permission was granted, with the caveat that he did not speak irreverently of the book. Doing so, he was warned, would bring "great damage" on him.

Mr. Bunyan was only granted liberty to give his first reason, namely, that the Common Prayer Book was not commanded in the Word of God. He was interrupted by the question from another of the justices as to whether or not there was a Scriptural commandment for Bunyan to go to either Elstow or Bedford. Bunyan replied that going to either town was a civil matter; and besides, God's calling allowed him to go wherever. But prayer was a part of the divine worship and was to be done according to the rule of God's Word.

Some of the justices appealed to Kelynge that Bunyan no longer be allowed to speak because he would cause harm. Kelynge responded that all those present need not fear, for they were learned and knew that the Common Prayer Book had existed since the time of the apostles. Bunyan interjected with the request that he be shown the place in the epistles where the prayer book was written or any text of Scripture that commanded him to use it. This evoked accusations against him from the justices. One asked if Bunyan's god was Beelzebub; others concluded that he was possessed "with the spirit of delusion, and of the devil."

The conversation then shifted to Bunyan's preaching. Kelynge confirmed the persuasion of the justices that Bunyan should not preach; whereupon,

Bunyan offered to prove his call to preach by the Scriptures. When Bunyan began to list the Scriptures, Kelynge limited him to the use of one text only. Bunyan quoted I Peter 4:10: *As every man hath received the gift, even so minister the same one to another...* Justice Kelynge interrupted with the interpretation of the text being that every man should follow his trade: "If any man hath received a gift of tinkering, as thou hast done, let him follow his tinkering."

Bunyan countered Kelynge that the text was most clearly referring to the preaching of the Word of God since the next verse explained the gift: *...if any man speak, let him speak as the oracles of God.* Kelynge responded that the text was limited to the instruction of each man's family in the private homes. Bunyan replied:

> *I said, If it was lawful to do good to some, it was lawful to do good to more. If it was a good duty to exhort our families, it is good to exhort others; but if they held it a sin to meet together to seek the face of God and exhort one another to follow Christ, I should sin still, for so we should do.*

At this confession of Bunyan, Justice Kelynge responded that he was not well-versed enough in the Scriptures to make responses to Bunyan. He and the other esteemed justices could spend no more time disputing with Bunyan. He asked Bunyan simply, "Then you confess the indictment; do you not?" At this moment, although not with certainty before, Bunyan wrote, "Now, and not till now, I saw I was indicted."

He confessed that he had been guilty of nothing else but meeting together with others to pray to God and exhort one another. He believed that they had had the "sweet comforting presence of the Lord among us for our encouragement." He plainly stated that he confessed himself guilty of nothing else.

Justice Kelynge ordered Bunyan to hear his judgment. Bunyan recounted the sentence in *A Relation of the Imprisonment of Mr. John Bunyan*:

> *You must be had back again to prison, and there lie for three months following; and at three months' end, if you do not submit to go to church to hear Divine service, and leave your preaching, you must be banished the realm; and if, after such a day as shall be appointed you to be gone, you shall be found in this realm, etc., or be found to come over again without special license from the king, etc., you must stretch by the neck for it, I tell you plainly...*

The jailer was instructed to take Bunyan away; but before he could be removed from the room, Bunyan responded to Kelynge's sentence: "I told him, as to this matter, I was at a point with him; for if I was out of prison today I would preach the Gospel again tomorrow, by the help of God."

Bunyan was prevented from hearing any responses from the justices by his brisk removal by the jailer. He wrote that he had been sweetly refreshed during his examination and that the words of the Lord Jesus Christ in Luke 21:15 had been to him more than "bare trifles": *I will give you a mouth and wisdom, which all your adversaries shall not be able to gainsay nor resist.* He concluded his recounting of the examination with his prayer: "The Lord make these profitable to all that shall read or hear them." He would later remember Sir John Kelynge particularly as Lord Hategood in Vanity Fair, *The Pilgrim's Progress.*

Elizabeth Bunyan and the four young Bunyan children were allowed a visit with John Bunyan. The events of the preceding weeks had left Bunyan resolute, but the strain and sorrow had exacted a heavy toll on Elizabeth who gave birth to a stillborn child. Through all her grief and hardship from Bunyan's long imprisonment, she remained steadfast and faithful, often taking Bunyan's food and soup herself to the jail.

On the third day of April 1661, as the twelve weeks drew to an end, Bunyan was visited by Mr. Paul Cobb. Cobb's visit was an official one. He came as the Clerk of the Peace and by the request of the magistrates to demand Bunyan to submit to the Church of England. Cobb warned Bunyan that if he refused to submit to the laws of the land, it would go worse with him at the next sessions. The justices intended to prosecute the laws against him if he did not forbear holding meetings.

Bunyan responded that the laws used against him had not been written to address meetings such as his. Those laws were meant to deal with those who had met under the guise of religion but actually for seditious purposes. The laws never intended to forbid private meetings where the worship of the Lord only was intended.

Cobb countered that everyone would refer to the past insurrection in London which had begun under the pretenses of religion but had ended in the overthrow of the kingdom.[22] Bunyan agreed that he was not in favor of such a practice; and that just because others had done such a thing, it did not follow that he intended to do so. He affirmed to Mr. Cobb his own loyalty to the king in both word and deed.

Many men of the times may have found this testimony of Bunyan's to be without merit or proof. No doubt it had been a point of recollection for Cobb and the justices that he had fought with the Parliamentary army and had worshiped as a Nonconformist the long years of Parliament rule. Those who were presiding over him as justices had remained true Royalists and had suffered for their positions, particularly Sir John Kelynge. John S. Roberts described Kelynge as "a cruel and tyrannical judge" who "exercised his authority over the Nonconformists with great sternness." This chiefjustice, according to Roberts, was a man of "loose and reckless character, and died despised and scorned by all good men, about a year before Bunyan was set at liberty."

Mr. Cobb cautioned Bunyan to seriously consider the matter. Bunyan quoted Cobb's admonition in his *Relation of Imprisonment*:

> *Well, said he, I do not profess myself to be a man that can dispute; but this I say truly,*

Neighbor Bunyan, I would have you consider this matter seriously, and submit yourself. You may have your liberty to exhort your neighbor in private discourse, so be you do not call together an assembly of people; and truly, you may do much good to the Church of Christ, if you would go this way; and this you may do and the law not abridge you of it. It is your private meetings that the law is against.

Bunyan told Cobb that he did not believe that Queen Elizabeth herself or her parliament had meant that the law forbade sincere religious meetings, only those meetings held under the pretense of religion. Here, Mr. Cobb spoke plainly to Bunyan's protest:

Very good; therefore the king, seeing that pretences are usually in and among the people, as to make religion their pretences only, therefore he, and the law before him, doth forbid such private meetings and tolerates only public; you may meet in public.

Bunyan's response was succinct:

And as for your saying I may meet in public, if I may be suffered, I would gladly do it; let me have but meetings enough in public, and I shall care the less to have them in private. I do not meet in private because I am afraid to have meetings in public.

Mr. Cobb then responded that Bunyan may attend public assemblies and listen. But he should not think himself to have received a gift above others and so be unwilling to hear other men preach. Cobb suggested that Bunyan sit still awhile to hear others and see how things would go for him. Bunyan answered that it was counted a sin for a man to refuse to preach:

> *Sir, said I, Wickliffe saith that he which leaveth off preaching and hearing of the word of God for fear of excommunication of men, he is already excommunicated of God, and shall in the day of judgment be counted a traitor to Christ.*

The obvious question from Cobb followed. "But," said he, "how shall we know that you have received a gift?" He asked if Bunyan would submit to the judgment of the Church to assess his calling to preach. Bunyan replied that he certainly would submit to the judgment of the Church of God. With that, Cobb concluded his endeavor to reason with Mr. Bunyan to submit to the laws:

> *Well, Neighbor Bunyan, said he, but indeed I would wish you seriously to consider of these things, between this and the quarter sessions, and to submit yourself. You may do much good if you continue still in the land; but, alas! what benefit will it be to your friends, or what good can it do to them, if you should be sent away beyond the seas into Spain, or Con-*

stantinople, or some other remote part of the world? Pray be ruled...the Scripture saith, 'The powers that be are ordained of God.'

Bunyan reminded Cobb of the Lord Jesus Christ before Pilate and Paul before the magistrates – that they both had recognized the authority of the rulers but were often imprisoned by those same rulers. Surely Mr. Cobb was not suggesting that either Christ or Paul had denied the authority of the magistrates and had sinned against God in disobedience of the law. He explained to Mr. Cobb:

Sir, said I, the law hath provided two ways of obeying: the one to do that which I in my conscience do believe that I am bound to do actively; and where I cannot obey actively, there I am willing to lie down and to suffer what they shall do unto me.

It was the custom to release different sorts of prisoners at the coronation of kings, and John Bunyan hoped he may be released at the coronation of Charles II on 23 April 1661. Although thousands were released, it was not to be for Bunyan. He was regarded as already having been convicted; therefore, his only recourse was to apply for pardon within twelve months of that conviction.

Biographer Ernest Bacon referred to a legal account written by Paul Cobb on 10 December 1670, sent to Roger Kenyon of Lancashire to be used as a precedent for similar cases.[23] Cobb wrote that Bunyan was indicted on a law from Elizabeth's rule.

When Bunyan had appeared in court, the indictment had been read to him; and although Bunyan had refused to plead to it, Cobb had been ordered to record Bunyan's confession. For that reason, Bunyan had still remained in prison. Conviction and sentencing were based on the rule of the Court, and Cobb believed that rule to be reasonable for anyone who appeared before the Court but refused to plead. The judgment should be rendered by *nihil dicit*. This is a Latin phrase meaning "he says nothing," which granted to the judge the authority to render a judgment against a defendant who refused to issue an answer against his own indictment or a plea within a prescribed time.

It is clear from this correspondence verifying legal precedence for that time that the courts believed John Bunyan had received a fair trial and was sentenced according to the law. He was to remain imprisoned until he submitted and conformed to the law.

A petition was prepared, but many believed that a conspiracy was afoot to keep Bunyan in prison. It was recommended that Elizabeth might visit Lord Barkwood in the House of Lords in London. After the difficult fifty-mile journey, her efforts were rewarded with the simple counsel that Bunyan could only be released by the judges of the assizes in Bedford.

The Midsummer Assizes in Bedford was held in August 1661 in the Chapel of Herne. Elizabeth was granted audience with Sir Matthew Hale, who had a reputation for sympathy for dissenters; but he offered her no hope. On the second day, she actually tossed a copy of the petition into the lap of Judge Twisdon as he rode in his coach. Angrily, he rebuked her, reminding her that her husband was convicted. She then visited Judge Hale a second time, but her meeting with Hale was overruled by Justice Chester who again reminded Elizabeth that her husband had been convicted. Encouraged by the high sheriff, Elizabeth went to a meeting of the judges and justices of the assizes in the Swan Chamber, an upper room in the Swan Inn. She again petitioned Matthew Hale, who assured her that he could do nothing since the justices had used what Bunyan had spoken at the previous session to bring a conviction against him. She protested that her husband had never confessed to the indictment and had never been lawfully convicted. Other of the justices protested that Bunyan's conviction was legal.

Elizabeth again replied in protest that "it was but a word of discourse that they took for a conviction." She was rebutted by Justice Chester who repeated that "it is recorded" as if his saying of it made the sentence truth. Once again she addressed Hale and the others, describing her journey to London and her meeting with Lord Barkwood who counseled her that her husband could be released by the justices at that assizes. "This he told me," she said, "and now I come to you to see if anything may be done in this business, and you give neither releasement nor relief."

The justices accused Bunyan of being "a pestilent fellow" and "a breaker of the peace." Would he leave off preaching was their demand. She answered that "he desired to live peaceably, to follow his calling, that his family might be maintained." Some conversation followed about Bunyan's proper calling as a tinker, rather than his calling as a preacher. At the agitation of the other justices, Hale, with some sympathy, told Elizabeth she had three options, namely, "either apply thyself to the king, or sue out his pardon, or get a writ of error; but a writ of error will be cheapest."

When Elizabeth realized that they had no intention of granting her request to call Bunyan and allow him to speak, she began to cry, not so much for their treatment of her, but because of the sad accounting they would give at the coming of the Lord when they would have to answer for all the things they had done.

Bunyan was not called to the following assizes in November 1661; but his jailer had already granted him some liberty, which he used to visit and minister to the people of God. With this bit of liberty, Bunyan even journeyed as far afield as London to visit Christians. The London excursions did not escape the notice of his enemies, and their threats to indict the poor jailer almost cost him his job. Bunyan was accused of visiting London with the intentions of plotting an insurrection and found himself kept more securely "so that I must not look out of the door."

By the time of the January 1662 assizes, Bunyan was so determined to be on the roster of cases called that he had his jailer write him on the list of felons. He had also made friends with the high sheriff and the judge, who promised that he would be called before the court. He was confident that all of these arrangements he had made would guarantee his appearance in court; but, as he wrote, "all was in vain."

Bunyan learned later that the Clerk of the Peace had been his worst enemy. In his *Relation* account, he did not name the clerk as the Paul Cobb who had been sent to persuade him the year before. But he did describe how this clerk accused the jailer of writing up a false calendar when listing the indictments of those to appear in court. The clerk retrieved the copies already sent to the judge and the high sheriff and blotted out Bunyan's accusation "as my jailer had writ it." The clerk then rewrote: "That John Bunyan was committed in prison, being lawfully convicted for upholding of unlawful meetings and conventicles..." To assure the success of his own intentions, the clerk then threatened the jailer with the payment of any fees that might be owed on Bunyan's account and the filing of a complaint against him for issuing false calendars.

And so began the long tedium of prison life that would become Bunyan's for the remainder of twelve years.

6

A Dreamer and an Author

Perhaps the enemies of John Bunyan intended to prevent another Cromwellian insurrection with Bunyan's conviction. Smaller, localized uprisings had occurred and had been squelched by the king's forces. But Bunyan's presence in the largeness of his physical appearance and the drawing power of his speech may have given his Royalist enemies cause for alarm. Bunyan's lack of formal education had not prevented his accumulation of just enough knowledge of the Holy Scriptures, they may have thought, to be dangerously used to stir up again the forces of the Dissenters who had not so long before removed the head of the king. Whatever the prevailing opinion actually was among the Royalists returned to power, it was obvious to them that Bunyan was a force with which to be reckoned; and reckon they did.

Nonconformists and dissenters of all kinds, including Quakers, were arrested as Clarendon's code of law began to tighten down the free movement of those opposing the episcopacy. The Bedford Church was forced to hold meetings in secret and in various places. If the object of those Royalists had been to keep Bunyan out of reach of other dissenting folks, then their mission had failed. Nonconformist meetings were disrupted, and worshipers were arrested at such a pace that Bunyan found himself cellmates with possibly sixty dissenters at one time. If Bunyan had aspired to be another

Cromwell, the best place for him should have been under lock and key. Yet, according to the testimony of one anonymous writer, Mr. Bunyan prayed and preached in those prison meetings with a great fullness of Divine persuasion.

Although necessity to provide for his family from his prison cell thrust upon him the new occupation of making long shoelaces for boots, his prison writing never waned. John Bunyan had become a published author before his arrest. But doubtless many will say that *The Pilgrim's Progress* would be the pinnacle of his creative work and the culmination of all his theological publications. Certainly it can be agreed that *The Pilgrim's Progress* and *The Holy War* would be Bunyan's consummate works of theology.

Young Bunyan and his pastor John Burton had been in debate with the Quakers in Bedford in 1656; and Bunyan's first published works, in 1656 and 1657, were responses to Quaker doctrines. His defense entitled *Some Gospel Truths Opened, according to the Scriptures, or the Divine and Human Nature of Jesus Christ* is seen written again in the description of Good-will at the Wicket Gate and again in the Interpreter's House, both in *The Pilgrim's Progress*:

> *This is Christ, who continually with the oil of his grace maintains the work already begun in the heart; by the means of which, notwithstanding what the devil can do, the souls of his people prove gracious still.*

With unarguable clarity, Bunyan wrote of the divine and human natures of Christ in his description of Prince Emmanuel, the Son of Shaddai in *The Holy War:*

> ...*that as Mansoul should in time be suffered to be lost so as certainly it should be recovered again. Recovered, I say, in such a way as that both the King and his Son would get themselves eternal fame and glory thereby...*

> ...*this Son of Shaddai, I say, having stricken hands with his Father, and promised that he would be his servant to recover his Mansoul again, stood by his resolution, nor would he repent of the same...that at a certain time prefixed by both, the King's Son should take a journey into the country of Universe, and there, in a way of justice and equity, by making amends for the follies of Mansoul, he should lay the foundation of her perfect deliverance...*

In 1658, after encouragement from the Bedford congregation, Bunyan published a sermon he had preached on the rich man and the beggar in Luke 16:19-31. His choice of title was considered "horrific" by one of his later biographers – *Sighs from Hell* or *The Groans of a Damned Soul;*[24] but the sermon itself is a lengthy exposition of the text by a young preacher who opened his preaching with the explanation of its purpose:

Friend, because it is a dangerous thing to be walking towards the place of darkness and anguish, and again, because it is...the journey that most of the poor souls in the world are taking, and that with delight and gladness, as if there was the only happiness to be found, I have therefore thought it my duty...for the preventing of thee...to tell thee, by opening this parable, what sad success those souls have had and are like to have that have been or shall be found persevering therein.

Bunyan again visited this subject in his allegorical sermon *The Pilgrim's Progress*. The introduction of Christian, a man under deep conviction of the wrath to come, is buffeted by his neighbors Obstinate and Pliable in the opening of *The Pilgrim's Progress*:

Then said the man, Neighbours, wherefore are ye come? They said, To persuade you to go back with us: but he said, That can by no means be: you dwell said he, in the city of Destruction...and dying there sooner or later, you will sink lower than the grave, into a place that burns with fire and brimstone. Be content, good neighbours, and go along with me.
What, said Obstinate, and leave our friends and our comforts behind us... Tush...away with your book; will you go back with us or no?

By May 1659, Bunyan's fourth publication had been printed. This was his theological consideration of the covenants of law and grace. The work was published under the title *The Doctrine of the Law and Grace Unfolded* and is an exposition of Romans 6:14: *For sin shall not have dominion over you: for ye are not under the law, but under grace.* Bunyan explained to the reader that true Gospel preaching must be a preaching together of both the Covenant of Works and the Covenant of Grace. Failure to preach the Law of God will prevent souls from understanding what they are by birth and consequently that they are condemned already, but failure to rightly preach the grace of the Gospel will not help souls to know God as He has communicated Himself in His grace and glory.

The soundness of this theology would be expounded from the depths of his own salvation experience to his dear readers in Christian's encounter with Worldly Wiseman in *The Pilgrim's Progress.* Dear Christian had been directed to the Wicket Gate by Evangelist. But directed on a much easier path by Mr. Worldly Wiseman, Christian climbed the high hill to Mr. Legality's house where the weight of the burden on his back increased and he "did quake for fear." As Christian then saw Evangelist approaching, Christian "began to blush for shame." Evangelist explained:

> *He to whom thou was sent for ease, being by name Legality, is the son of the bondwoman, which now is in bondage with her children...Now if she with her children are in*

bondage, how canst thou expect by them to be made free?

After this, Evangelist called aloud to the heavens for confirmation of what he had said; and with that there came words and fire out of the mountain under which poor Christian stood, that made the hair of his flesh stand up: the words were thus pronounced, "As many as are of the works of the law, are under the curse..."

During the months of 1661, Bunyan wrote five letters to the Bedford congregation relating the facts of his trial and imprisonment thus far. These letters were published in 1765 under the title *A Relation of the Imprisonment of Mr. John Bunyan.* In those early days of prison confinement, he wrote *Christian Behaviour* on the fruits of true Christianity and also *Prison Meditations,* a lengthy poem dedicated both to "suffering saints and reigning sinners" saved by grace, and published in 1665.

I am (indeed) in prison now
In body, but my mind
Is free to study Christ, and how
Unto me he is kind.

For tho' men keep my outward man
Within their locks and bars,
Yet by the faith of Christ I can
Mount higher than the stars.

In 1664, the Conventicle Act had passed. All religious meetings were outlawed, except those of the Established Church of England. The Five Mile Act passed in 1665. This notorious law forbade Nonconformists from preaching or teaching in schools or to live within five miles of any incorporated town where they had preached. Hundreds of men were deprived of their pulpits and incomes and banished from their communities. Yet Bunyan's pen was never idle; nor did he lack a printer willing to print Nonconformist literature.[25]

In 1665, publications of *The Holy City* and *The Resurrection of the Dead* as well as two poems – *Ebal and Gerizim* and *Prison Meditations* – were printed. But it was in this year also that the Great Plague once again visited London. By July, many Londoners had left the city; and Parliament had moved to Oxford. By 1666, the plague was carried to the surrounding areas, including Bedford and Newport Pagnell. Matthias Cowley, Bunyan's old friend from military days and bookseller in Newport Pagnell, died in the plague.[26] Some ejected Nonconformist ministers who had been restricted by the Five Mile Act returned to London to preach and minister to those left in the city.

The Great Fire of London spread through the city in September 1666. Some of the first printings of *Grace Abounding to the Chief of Sinners* were destroyed, making copies of the first edition very rare. It is in this publication of Bunyan's autobiography that much is learned about his own spiritual struggles. *Grace Abounding* was written, as Bunyan penned, for those who had come to faith under his preaching:

> *Written by the author, and dedicated to those whom God hath counted him worthy to beget to faith by his ministry in the Word.*

His pastoral duties of teaching and oversight were greatly hindered by his confinement, but his pen and the printed page made a mighty pulpit of edification for those left bereft of ministerial leadership. He spoke again in *Grace Abounding*:

> *I have sent you here enclosed a drop of that honey that I have taken out of the carcass of a lion. I have eaten thereof myself, and am much refreshed thereby. (Temptations, when we meet them at first, are as the lion that roared upon Samson; but if we overcome them, the next time we see them, we shall find a nest of honey within them.)*

For some brief time after the Great Fire, Bunyan was released from jail, according to a biography written by his friend Charles Doe. Doe wrote that Bunyan was re-arrested again at a meeting and returned to jail "where he lay six years more." The sadness of this confinement was compounded by the death of his blind daughter Mary. Bunyan was left alone to sell his tagged shoelaces at the prison gate.

Beginning in April 1670, the Second Conventicle Act caused another harsh persecution of Nonconformists, including the arrest of members of the Bedford congregation. It was in May of that year that King Charles secretly signed the Treaty of Dover, entering into an alliance with the king of France to re-establish England in Roman Catholicism. This would prove favorable for Bunyan.

Although two books were published, Bunyan's pen was not as prolific during this second term of imprisonment. But in November 1671, the buffeted congregation of Bedford called and elected John Bunyan to be their pastor. Seven godly men were also elected to assist Bunyan in preaching and ministerial work in the surrounding villages.

King Charles began to implement maneuvers to enact his intentions for his signing of the Treaty of Dover. His Declaration of Indulgence in 1672 allowed leniency to be granted to Roman Catholics, Quakers, and Nonconformists. Sometime early in 1672, under the terms of this Declaration, Bunyan was released. He was given a license to preach in May, which he was required to produce for civil authorities when preaching away from home. The Bedford congregation, no longer needing to meet in secret, purchased a barn to be used for the church meeting place.

It was during this period of liberty that Bunyan suffered written attacks from some of the Established Church clergy. He also suffered accusations of improper behavior concerning an unmarried lady in the congregation. These attacks he rebutted in a later printing of *Grace Abounding*. But his family was enlarged during this time by the birth of daughter Sarah and then son Joseph.

The political winds began shifting again with Parliament's passage of the Test Act in 1673. The political climate steadily worsened until Charles succumbed to Parliamentary tightening of the purse strings; and in February 1675, he officially declared preaching licenses issued under the Declaration of Indulgence to be null and void. Thus began another time of persecution for Nonconformists and Dissenters.

Bunyan was warned of a warrant issued for his arrest in March 1675.[27] His refusal to attend the Established Church and partake of the sacrament had provided the bishop with a *writ de excommunicato capiendo*. This law, dating from Elizabeth's reign, allowed the sheriff to arrest anyone who failed to attend the services and the sacraments of the Established Church.

Although Bunyan remained in hiding for some months, he was not prevented from issuing two publications. His sermon *Light for Them that Sit in Darkness* was put into print as was a catechism of the lengthy puritanical title *Instruction for the Ignorant; being a Salve to cure that great want of Knowledge in both Old and Young*. The public was further instructed that this catechism had been prepared in "a plain and easy dialogue, fitted to the capacity of the weakest." But Bunyan addressed his target audience in his introduction – "To the Church of Christ in and about Bedford." Never shirking his responsibilities, he committed to writing those doctrinal teachings he would have faithfully administered in person had he been permitted. "I could do no less (being driven from you in presence, not affection)," he lamented, "but first present you with this little book..." In true pastoral counsel, he urged them to remember the blessed truths and to use the book to witness to family members yet without Christ. He then addressed all the unconverted who had heard him preach but who yet remained in their sins: "I entreat them also that they receive it as a token of my love to their immortal souls." His love was always the vehicle by which he warned the unrepentant of judgment to come: "I charge them, as they will answer in the day of terrible judgment, that they read, ponder, and receive this wholesome medicine prepared for them."

Bunyan was able to evade arrest, by the help of his friends, until the late autumn of 1676, when he was again taken to the Bedford jail. Some of his Nonconformist friends knew of a law that would allow two people to offer a cautionary bond to the bishop on behalf of a prisoner detained under that old Elizabethan law and to petition for his release. The esteemed Dr. John Owen, another of Bunyan's friends, spoke on behalf of Bunyan before Thomas Barlow the Bishop of Lincoln. The bond was accepted on the testimony of Dr. Owen and other Nonconformist friends; and in June 1677, Bunyan was released.

The year following would be the year of greatest renown for the esteemed preacher of Bedford jail. *The Pilgrim's Progress*, Bunyan's most famous book, was published by Nathaniel Ponder in February 1678. Mystery surrounds the date of the writing of the book. Dr. John Brown, a Bedford pastor and 19th century Bunyan biographer, believed

Bunyan dreamed the dream of this famous allegory that evening in December 1676, when he resumed his residency as a prisoner in Bedford jail.[28]

However, biographer John S. Roberts quoted Robert Southey in an 1873 biography of Bunyan: "...the germ of the 'Pilgrim's Progress' is to be found in a dream...recorded in 'Grace Abounding'..." In his youthful days of his agonizing perplexity and searching to know Christ, Bunyan had had a dream of the state of happiness he himself had witnessed among the poor folk in Bedford. In his dream, the townsfolk were refreshing themselves on a sunny side of a high mountain while he was shivering in the cold on the other side. It seemed he was divided from them by a high wall that went around the mountain. In his earnest desire to join them on the other side, he tried, without success, to find a way through the wall. At last he found a tiny doorway of such narrow proportions that he was unable to get through in spite of all his efforts. Yet, after considerable struggle and discomfort, he squeezed through and joined the happy throng.

Bunyan explained the meaning of this allegorical dream in *Grace Abounding*. The mountain was the Church with the sun of God's merciful face shining upon them. The Bible was the wall that separated those Christians from the world; and the door was the Lord Jesus Christ – the only Way to the Father. (John 14:6) The narrowness of the door showed Bunyan that "none could enter into life, but those that were in downright earnest, and unless also they left that wicked world behind them; for here was only room for body and soul, but not for body and soul, and sin."

His prolific pen had not run dry as Bunyan had faithfully applied himself to recording his sermons and other writings. It is probable that he was engaged in the preparation of another book which he laid aside to write down the story he had dreamed. The reader of this allegory would be satisfied to account for its story as the fruits of more than one dream; but without a doubt, reminisces of his dream of that mountain scene shaped the outset of Christian's journey.

Rather than in the form of a sermon, this story that had intruded itself upon his mind would be written as an allegory. He explained in his *Apology* introducing *The Pilgrim's Progress:*

> *When at the first I took my pen in hand*
> *Thus for to write, I did not understand*
> *That I at all should make a little book*
> *In such a mode: nay, I had undertook*
> *To make another; which, when almost done,*
> *Before I was aware I this begun.*
>
> *And thus it was: I writing of the way*
> *And race of saints in this our gospel day,*
> *Fell suddenly into an allegory*
> *About their journey and the way to glory*

Whether the book was both begun and concluded in this imprisonment is not agreed upon by all of his biographers. But Bunyan verified that at least a great portion was indeed written in his den, as he called his prison, described in his introduction:

> *As I walked through the wilderness of this world, I lighted on a certain place where was a den, and laid me down in that place to sleep; and as I slept, I dreamed a dream.*

As he launched forth into the tale of Christian and his journey to the Celestial City, Bunyan was penning one of the most extraordinary books of theology. Dr. John P. Gulliver wrote in his Introduction to the 1882 edition of *The Complete Works of John Bunyan*: "No man can thoroughly understand the *Pilgrim's Progress* without becoming an accomplished theologian." The immediate and sustained success of the book Dr. Gulliver attributed to "its presentation of truth." Bunyan said as much: "My dark and cloudy words, they do but hold the truth, as cabinets enclose the gold."

The writer of the Introduction of a very early copy of *The Pilgrim's Progress* published by the American Tract Society described this as a "book which has done as much good, perhaps, as any other, except the Bible" and the book which made Bunyan more useful than if "he had enjoyed the unrestrained exercise of his public ministry." This unidentified biographer continued his commentary on *The Pilgrim's Progress*:

> *In composing it, he was evidently favored with a peculiar measure of the Divine assistance. Within the confines of a jail, he was able so to delineate the Christian's course, with*

its various difficulties, perils, and conflicts, that scarcely any thing seems to have escaped his notice.

The Reverend John Baillie in his *Life Studies: or How to Live* described Bunyan as "his own Pilgrim embodied into life." Dr. Gulliver described all of Bunyan's works as a "transcript of his own experience." Bunyan wrote, as Dr. Gulliver asserted, "what *he had himself experienced.*" Apart from the Word of God, a writer's best source is often his own experience. The story he can weave or lessons he can teach spring from his own personal wealth of living. Bunyan himself had grown older while imprisoned, but he had also grown wiser. The walls of Bedford jail had been privy to his personal struggles, his griefs, and his joys. This oft solitude and the deprivation of prison life had honed and polished Bunyan's theology, discarding pettiness and pampering for the exquisiteness of gems. Each written jewel can still be held glimmering in the light of God's Word to reveal the Lord Jesus Christ in His resplendent beauty. How are His people to be holy even as He is holy? Bunyan's deft pen details the cutting and chipping, the buffing and polishing required.

"Prick him anywhere, and he bleeds the Bible," was the common description of John Bunyan by many, including the eminent Baptist Charles Spurgeon. And so it is true with Bunyan. Springing up from the deepest well of his personal experience, Bunyan lays aside the unnecessary and cuts to the quick of the Christian's walk with Christ. This is not the Christian's world. Here we are pilgrims traveling to the Celestial City.

7

A Freed Man and a Free Man

After twelve years, John Bunyan left the Bedford jail a freed man. He had received a royal pardon for a crime he had never owned from the man whose religious ambition had squelched the free proclamation of God's Word since his ascendency to the throne. Such a blemish remains to mar the complexion of a country whose citizens had secured liberties from the crown granted in that "Great Charter of the Liberties" of 1215.

Perhaps it had only been a political myth that the glorious Magna Carta had guaranteed certain individual political rights, but English jurists of the 17th century had invoked its tenets in their stance against the injustices of the Stuart monarchs. Bunyan himself had fought in the Parliamentary army in support of individual liberty. But he had fallen victim to the second Charles's invocation of the divine right of kings and the degradation of his own citizen rights to have quick justice and to be kept from illegal imprisonment. Equally as devastating for Bunyan and his suffering contemporaries – religious freedom, so gloriously attained and afforded for a few brief years, was unjustly revoked. They had tasted such blessed liberty to pray and to preach; to forego its practice was unthinkable. To be bound to prayers prescribed by other men was unconscionable – a prison for the soul. It was a choice they could not make.

As Bunyan explained in *Grace Abounding*, "I was indicted for an upholder and maintainer of unlawful assemblies and conventicles, and for not conforming to the national worship of the Church of England." His indictment remains astonishing when it is considered where and by whom he was arrested. Reverend George Cheever aptly framed the reminder that it was "in a Christian land, by an Established Church, for preaching the Gospel to the poor, the ignorant, the destitute, and for not praying with a Common Prayer Book!" Bunyan's surprising indictment and sentencing seemed to be an all-in-one event, as he related:

> *After some conference there with the justices, they taking my plain dealing with them for a confession, as they termed it, of the indictment, did sentence me to a perpetual banishment, because I refused to conform.*

But Bunyan's heart had been prepared in the months prior to his arrest. "Before I came to prison, I saw what was a-coming," he wrote, "and had especially two considerations warm upon my heart." His first fear was the understandable fear of how he would face death. Here the Lord met his need with the comfort of Colossians 1:11: *...strengthened with all might, according to his glorious power, unto all patience and longsuffering with joyfulness.* His second grave concern was for the care of his family. Here the Lord provided the text of II Corinthians 1:9: *But we had the sentence of death in ourselves, that we should not trust ourselves, but in God which* *raiseth the dead.* He was made to understand that proper suffering required that he "must first pass a sentence of death upon everything that can properly be called a thing of this life...all, as dead to me, and myself as dead to them."

Yet Bunyan confessed that he was "a man encompassed with infirmities." His parting with his wife and children was "as the pulling the flesh from my bones" when he thought about their hardships and miseries resulting from his imprisonment. His heart was particularly tender toward his blind daughter Mary, and thoughts of her personal suffering plagued him sorely. Then he "thought on those two milch kine that were to carry the ark of God into another country, and to leave their calves behind them." (I Samuel 6:10) He resigned Mary and the rest of his family to the care of the Lord.

As the years of confinement passed for Bunyan, his times of trial and testing often sank him to depths that fluctuated his resolve; but Christ's faithfulness to apply the balm of the Word never wavered. His fear of banishment caused him to seek more earnestly for God. He grappled with his own imaginings of what banishment required and even with the Scriptures that described the sufferings of the saints.

> *I have verily thought that my soul and it have sometimes reasoned about the sore and sad estate of a banished and exiled condition – how they are exposed to hunger, to cold, to perils, to nakedness, to enemies, and a thousand*

calamities; and at last it may be to die in a ditch, like a poor forlorn and desolate sheep.

One such trial of facing death left him for some time in the clutches of his own personal Giant Despair as he contemplated the possibility that his confinement would end on the gallows. "I thought," he confessed in *Grace Abounding*:

> *...that in the condition I now was in I was not fit to die, neither indeed did think I could, if I should be called to it: besides, I thought with myself, if I should make a scrabbling shift to clamber up the ladder, yet I should, either with quaking, or other symptoms of faintings give occasion to the enemy to reproach the way of God and His people for their timorousness.*

He was often so obsessed with the thought of dying that he would picture himself "as if I was on the ladder with a rope about my neck." But in true Bunyan style, he was consoled with the thought that a hanging would draw a large crowd to whom he could preach the Gospel; and perhaps one soul would be converted with his last words. Then he would not consider his life as "thrown away nor lost."

But still, as he described, "the Tempter followed me" badgering him with doubts and requiring evidences of his claim on Christ. At last, he said, "That it was for the Word and way of God that I was in this condition; wherefore I was engaged not to flinch a hair's breadth from it." He would later incorporate his own warfare with his fears in Christian's confrontation with Apollyon in the Valley of Humiliation:

> *Then did Christian begin to be afraid, and to cast in his mind whether to go back or stand his ground. But he considered again that he had no armour for his back, and therefore thought that to turn the back to him might give him greater advantage, with ease to pierce him with his darts. Therefore he resolved to venture, and stand his ground...*

Bunyan's fears found quick rebukes by the administration of Scripture following Scripture. And so like Christian to Hopeful:

> *What a fool, quoth he, am I, thus to lie in a stinking dungeon when I may as well walk at liberty: I have a key in my bosom called Promise, that will, I am persuaded, open any lock in Doubting Castle.*

His resolve did not open the lock on his literal prison door, but it gave him the freedom of soul and mind to submit to the way of God's intended usefulness for him. He described this resolve in *Grace Abounding*:

> *I thought also, that God might choose whether He would give me comfort now, or at the hour of death, but I might not therefore choose whether I would hold my profession or*

no. I was bound, but He was free...wherefore, thought I...I am for going on and venturing my eternal state with Christ, whether I have comfort here or no.

In the comfort afforded to his heart, he testified that never in his life had the Scriptures been made more plain to him nor the Lord Jesus Christ more real to him as within the confines of his prison. Even in his long confinement, he had "continued with much content through grace" and had "received among many things, much conviction, instruction, and understanding."

All the long, weary months of agony, striving to know the blessed comfort of Christ had earned John Bunyan a prison sentence for living in obedience to that blessed Comfort he had finally come to know. But the way for Bunyan was the perfect way of the all-wise God who teaches each one *in the way that He shall choose* (Psalm 25:12). Those who had intended to silence him only provided a grander pulpit. In their attempt to restrict him, they had provided him time for reflection and study to preach in his writings to an innumerable host in a congregation spanning centuries.

They could not silence such a force of God. His sermons and admonitions and allegories issued forth from the fertile ground of a mind steeped in Scripture and molded by experience. He was the "man of a very stout countenance" Christian saw in the house of the Interpreter, who had said, "Set down my name, Sir." And then, Bunyan, as did that man, drew his sword, put on his helmet, and rushed upon the armed men at the door, fiercely cutting and hacking until he had "pressed forward into the palace" – the perfect picture of Acts 14:22: *...that we must through much tribulation enter into the kingdom of God.*

Reverend George Cheever wrote in his 1845 biography: "There never was a man, who made better use of his temptations..." Bunyan was a man who not only made "better use" of his temptations, but also made "better use" of his trials. These were not forces of destruction in his life; but rather, by them, he was sent to the Scriptures. The continuance and the co-mingling of testing and temptation brought forth gems for the edification of the Church. Bunyan wrote at least sixty books in his lifetime; but if he had spent the twelve years confined to write *The Pilgrim's Progress* alone, the benefit is incalculable. In his youthful days of searching, he had been left with the Scriptures alone and, eventually, *Luther's Commentaries on Galatians.* In his prison days, his constant companions were his Bible and his copy of *Foxe's Book of Martyrs.* Consequently, *The Pilgrim's Progress*, as Cheever described, " is as a piece of rich tapestry" which Bunyan wove "into one beautiful picture the various spiritual scenery and thrilling events of his own life...as a Christian pilgrim."

The power of the written word reigned supreme in the days Bunyan took up his own pen to write. His literary genius was rooted in his ability to paint with words so brilliantly common and yet encompassing the gamut of the spoken English language of his day. He wrote in each sermon and allegory equally for educated and uneducated. His biographer in the 1880 *Elstow Edition* of *The Pilgrim's Progress* quoted the interesting fact that *The Pilgrim's Progress* has whole pages of words that never exceed two syllables. Bunyan explained his style in his own words:[29]

> *Words easy to be understood do often hit the mark, when high and learned ones do only pierce the air. He also that speaks to the weakest, may make the learned understand him; when he that striveth to be high, is not only for the most part understood but of a sort, but also many times is neither understood by them nor by himself.*

Puritan theologians are known for their wringing every morsel of thought out of a text. Bunyan, as a theologian, was true to his Puritan contemporaries. In his sermons, Bunyan picked the bone clean in sucking out every morsel of nourishment from the text. No liberty is given to add to Scripture; but as Bunyan said in *The Holy War,* we can pick out every meaning.

> *Then stood up my Lord Mayor, whose name was my Lord Understanding, and he began to pick and pick, until he had picked comfort out of that seemingly bitter saying of the Lord Secretary...because none of his words were such, but that at all times they were most exactly significant; and the townsmen were allowed to pry into them...*

Bunyan was a master of the allegory. Some have agreed with George Cheever that Bunyan's allegory was not conformed to the poetic rules but rather was his own universal language of allegory. Some would say that *The Holy War* is equal in quality and beauty with *The Pilgrim's Progress*. The two allegories could be compared to different sides of the same coin. *The Pilgrim's Progress* might be understood as the description of the externals of a Christian life while *The Holy War* would be understood as manifesting the internal work in the Christian life. Reverend Robert Maguire described *The Holy War* as "A History of the Human Soul" that "deals with the inward struggles of the soul, and thence proceeds to the outer consequences." He described *The Pilgrim's Progress* as a progression from the external circumstances of the "Christian Pilgrimage" to the inner experiences of the Christian.

The esteemed Puritan genius John Milton published his first version of his epic poem *Paradise Lost* in 1667 while Bunyan was writing in confinement in Bedford jail. As the number of Bunyan's publications grew, so did the esteem for his ability to bridge the gaps of young and old, cultivated and working class, converted and unconverted and to crack the hull that the kernel of knowledge could be palatable for all. With the publication of his *The Pilgrim's Progress*, Bunyan would earn esteem and renown, ranking him with John Milton. The beauty of Bunyan's work was the accessibility and commonality of his language that allowed him to create his own style of poetic allegory. George Cheever wrote of Bunyan's poetry: "He is indeed the only Poet, whose genius was nourished entirely by the Bible. He felt and thought in Scripture imagery."

Bunyan spoke himself of his intentions in putting pen to paper:

> *I writing of the way*
> *And race of saints in this our gospel day,*
> *Fell suddenly into an allegory,*
> *About their journey and the way to glory...*
>
> *This book will make a traveler of thee,*
> *If by its counsels thou wilt ruled be;*
> *It will direct thee to the Holy Land,*
> *If thou wilt its directions understand;*
> *Yea, it will make the slothful active be;*
> *The blind also delightful things to see.*

But *The Pilgrim's Progress* is truly a book of practical theology – a simple study of the Triune God in relationship with His people. Oftentimes the plainness of Scripture is hard to bear; and when the winds of memory shake loose the fruits of experience, the remembrance of the pain of personal attempts to mend a vessel broken by sin needs the balm of God's Word. Bunyan's genius shines in this capacity to apply the ointment of the Word to the hurting brokenness of despair. In gentleness, his characters speak to the wounded heart with refreshment and encouragement. He writes of his story:

> *Wouldst thou divert thyself from melancholy?...Oh then come hither! And lay my book, thy head, and heart together.*

Never did Bunyan dilute the justice of the Law nor the consequences for refusing mercy. Never did he slight the royal prerogative of Shaddai and Prince Emmanuel as he affirmed in *The Holy War*:

> *For we are resolved, if in peaceable manner you do not submit yourselves, then to make a war upon you, and to bring you under by force.*

But always he laid the terrors of the Law alongside the promises of Grace. Again he wrote in *The Holy War*:

> *O Mansoul, is it little in thine eyes that our King doth offer thee mercy, and that after so many provocations? Yea, he still holdeth out his golden scepter to thee, and will not yet suffer his gate to be shut against thee: wilt thou provoke him to do it?*   *– Captain Judgment*

> *When Mr. Desires-Awake saw the Prince, he fell flat with his face to the ground, and cried out, "Oh, that Mansoul might live before thee!" and with that he presented the petition; the which when the Prince had read, he turned away for a while and wept; but refraining himself, he turned again to the man, who all this while lay crying at his feet, as at the first, and*

said to him, "Go thy way to thy place, and I will consider of thy requests."

– Prince Emmanuel

The dynamic genius of Bunyan flourished from the support of his own testimony. He preached what he himself had lived. His written testimony repeated in all of his writings remains the verbal affirmation that God's Word is the all-sufficient truth that grants a remedy to every need. His inner struggles belong personally to every seeking soul. His steadfastness in his sufferings affirms to every believer the promise of the Lord Jesus: *"...my grace is sufficient for thee"* (II Corinthians 12:9). To Bunyan, Christ was preeminent; and all his conversation "was about the Lord of the hill."

Bunyan's common-sense wisdom instructs new converts as well as reminds seasoned pilgrims. John S. Roberts believed that formal theological education would have "narrowed his influence and weakened his power." Roberts described Bunyan's writings as "distinguished by their force and simplicity." One such example is his candid and descriptive warnings of false professors and deceivers illustrated in Christian's discourse with Faithful about Mr. Talkative:

I will give you a further discovery of him. This man is for any company, and for any talk: as he talketh now with you, so will he talk when he is on the ale-bench...Religion hath no place in his heart, or house, or conversation: all he hath lieth in his tongue; and his religion is to make a noise therewith. – Christian to Faithful

This brings to my mind that of Moses, by which he described the beast that is clean, (Lev. xi; Deut. xiv.) – he is such an one that parteth the hoof and cheweth the cud; not that parteth the hoof only, or that cheweth the cud only...this truly resembleth Talkative; he cheweth the cud, he seeketh knowledge! He cheweth upon the word; but he divideth not the hoof, but he parteth not with the way of sinners... – Faithful to Christian

Bunyan's freedom did not stem the flow of publications even while maintaining his busy preaching and pastoral schedule. *A Treatise of the Fear of God* was published in 1679, followed by *The Life and Death of Mr. Badman* in 1680. A fraudulent Part II of *The Pilgrim's Progress* was published in 1682 and was exposed by Bunyan's printer Nathaniel Ponder. In that same year, *The Holy War* was published; and again, Bunyan employed his own homespun allegorical style to tell the story of Mansoul:

*Then lend thine ear to what I do relate,
Touching the town of Mansoul and her state:
How she was lost, took captive, made a slave;
And how against Him set that should her save.*

The Holy War, considered among Bunyan's voluminous works, would rank second only to *The*

Pilgrim's Progress. Lord Thomas Macaulay famously remarked that it would be the greatest English language allegory if *The Pilgrim's Progress* had not been written. The story of *The Holy War* relates the losing and taking again of the town of Mansoul staged as a medieval fortress town whose five gates opened only from the inside. Bunyan's knowledge of medieval military strategies and warfare embellished the narrative and lent strength to the plot itself – the fall and redemption of man – as he described "when 'twas set up and when pulling down."

Opening *The Holy War*, Bunyan penned an "Advertisement to the Reader" denying claims of plagiarism leveled against him concerning the plot and text of *The Pilgrim's Progress*:

> *Some say the Pilgrim's Progress is not mine,*
> *Insinuating as if I would shine*
> *In name and fame by the worth of another,*
> *Like some made rich by robbing of their brother.*

While he was confessing his true authorship of the first allegory, he concluded by verifying his true authorship of *The Holy War*:

> *Also for this thine eye is now upon,*
> *The matter in this manner came from none*
> *But the same heart and head, fingers and pen*
> *As did the other. Witness all good men:*
> *For none in all the world, without a lie,*

Can say that "this is mine," excepting I.

In spite of the spurious copy of a Part II of *The Pilgrim's Progress*, Bunyan's audience eagerly awaited a sequel. After all, he had left them in suspense when he concluded the first: "I know not but 'twill make me dream again." In 1684, he delighted his readers with a genuine Part II and blessed their consternation over Christian's family with the relation of the journey to the Celestial City of Christiana and her children. John Newton wrote in the preface to an early edition of these two works combined that Bunyan's writings really needed no "recommendatory preface." Newton granted that Part II included "many beautiful passages that sufficiently demonstrate it to be the work of the same masterly hand"; but he did not consider the second part to, in any way, compete with the first part. Part II deserves to be read; and explanatory notes on the first will be keys to understanding the second part.

A note of caution may be included on the various parts of *The Pilgrim's Progress*. John Newton offered a caution in his own preface. A Part III began to be circulated and annexed to American editions of Part I and Part II. Although this Part III bore the name of Bunyan as the author, Newton ruled it "a gross imposition and forgery."[30]

In February 1685, King Charles II died. As was to be expected in such days of political wrangling, his death stirred again a time of intrigue and uncertainty. James II ascended the throne, nursing his brother's former ambition to return England to Roman Catholicism. The renewed sufferings of

Nonconformists aroused Bunyan's concern for his tenuous liberty and prompted him to commit his last will and testament to writing, granting all his possessions to his wife Elizabeth Bunyan. This Deed of Gift was duly witnessed and deposited safely in the chimney place of their cottage. Frank Mott Harrison noted in his biography that Elizabeth evidently never retrieved the document, and it was not found again until the cottage was being demolished in 1838.[31]

Bunyan published *A Book for Boys and Girls: Or, Country Rhimes for Children* in 1686, yet it appears that he devoted his time to preaching and pastoring for the next two years. His London friend Charles Doe noted that his fame as a preacher gathered large crowds whenever he filled the pulpit as a visiting minister. Doe recorded that only one day's notice would be needed for twelve hundred people to attend an early meeting on a dark winter morning workday. But fame was not enticing for Bunyan. The heart of his ministry remained in Bedford.

The year 1688 would be a full year for John Bunyan. Once again, he had been occupied with writing and had published five books in that year. But the birth of a Catholic heir to King James II spurred an invitation to the Dutch Protestant William of Orange to come to England. With the backdrop of political uncertainties that year, Bunyan faithfully continued to minister.

In August, he was called to Reading to arbitrate a family dispute; after which, he journeyed on horseback to London carrying in his pocket the manuscript of *The Acceptable Sacrifice*. After spending the night in Reading, he continued his journey to London in a torrential downpour of rain. He arrived at John Strudwick's house wet and cold and remained resting at Mr. Strudwick's until the Lord's Day morning of August 19th. He was not well but insisted on preaching, as promised, at Mr. Gammons' meeting-house at White-chapel. Already ill, he preached what was to be his last sermon and returned to Mr. Strudwick's.

For ten days, Bunyan lay wracked with fever, until the early morning of 31 August 1688. Gathered around his bed were his friends – the minister George Cokayn and his other friends Charles Doe and John Strudwick. His grief in life had often been his language of prayer. But this was his blessed meeting day to see the One he had served so faithfully. In his own words from *One Thing is Needful*, his anticipation and joy in that answered prayer is described:

> *What gladness shall possess our heart*
> *When we shall see these things!*
> *What light and life in every part*
> *Will rise like lasting springs!*
>
> *Oh blessed face and holy grace!*
> *When shall we see this day?*
> *Lord, fetch us to this goodly place,*
> *We humbly do thee pray.*

He had already written his farewell to his dearly beloved Church at Bedford in his dedicatory preface to *Grace Abounding*:

My Dear Children:

The milk and honey are beyond this wilderness. God be merciful to you, and grant that you be not slothful to go in to possess the land.

JOHN BUNYAN.

John Bunyan was indeed a free man.

Epilogue

"A truly religious life is always a secret life: it is a life hid, as Paul has it, with Christ in God," so wrote the esteemed Scottish divine Alexander Whyte in his *Bunyan's Characters*. Bunyan had well understood the secret intimacy of Christ with His saints. He knew well, too, the meaning of Psalm 25:14: *The secret of the Lord is with them that fear him; and he will shew them his covenant.* It was Secret whom Bunyan dispatched with a message from the Merciful One:

> *My name is Secret; I dwell with those that are high...the Merciful One hath sent me to tell thee that he is a God ready to forgive, and that he taketh delight to multiply to pardon offences.*

In Dr. Whyte's estimation, Bunyan's "whole soul lay naked and open to the eyes of his sanctified imagination" until his spiritual life became more real to him than the realities of life around him. Dr. Whyte wrote of Bunyan's secret religious life:

> *In the divine preparation of the author of the Pilgrim's Progress, both in his great conversion, and alongside of his great life of sanctification, his wonderful imagination was always working...and it was all taken up into the hand of the Holy Ghost and was turned continually in upon the terrible battle between sin*

and grace that went on incessantly in Bunyan's mind and heart and life.

But the secret spiritual struggles of Bunyan formed the roots of one who grew into such a mighty oak of Christian stature that his branches still overspread and drop with sweet benefits on saints today who read his works. The secrets of Bunyan's heart became his message proclaimed abroad to the incalculable edification of those both near to him and far distantly removed. He understood the graces of faith, hope, and love that accompany salvation and reap the bountiful fruit of the Spirit. These graces he depicted in his "five pickt men" so named by Dr. Whyte from Bunyan's own marginal note in *The Holy War*: "'Five graces pickt out of an abundance of common virtues.'"

> *Well, you see how I have told you that the King's Son was engaged to come from the court to save Mansoul, and that his Father had made him the Captain of the forces…five noble captains and their forces…Captain Credence, Captain Good-hope, Captain Charity, Captain Innocent, Captain Patience…*

But to that small company of men gathered around the bedside of their dear, dying friend that early August morning, consolation came only in knowing that John Bunyan was at rest. In their grief, they made preparations for his burial. John Strudwick provided the vault; and Bunyan's body was laid to rest in Bunhill Fields near Aldersgate –

the resting place for many esteemed Nonconformists, including Bunyan's dear friend Dr. John Owen. Among these venerable dead and in the presence of mourners from the London Nonconformist congregations, Bunyan was buried on the third day of September 1688, with his beloved friend George Cokayn conducting the service.

When news of Bunyan's death reached his family and his congregation, a day of prayer was called for that first week and the week following and again the third week. The congregation felt the heavy and sorrowful loss of their beloved pastor.

John Bunyan had wisely recorded his provision for his wife and children, but no mention is made of Elizabeth executing her husband's will. It seems, from accounts, that a fruitless search for the Deed of Gift required an administration of the estate to be jointly accomplished by Elizabeth and two of Bunyan's friends in Bedford. The whole lot of his goods and substance and the cottage was given to Elizabeth and the children. There she lived until her death in 1691.

George Cokayn, the London pastor and friend, was given the manuscript, carried by Bunyan in his pocket, teaching of that acceptable sacrifice of a contrite heart. Bunyan had spent his first days of that last journey to London completing the text of *The Acceptable Sacrifice* with the intention of delivering it to the printer. It would indeed go to the printer in that September 1688, but by the hand of George Cokayn, who first penned a tribute and admonishment in his Preface to the Reader:

The author of the ensuing discourse – now with God, reaping the fruit of all his labour, diligence, and success, in his Master's service – did experience in himself, through the grace of God, the nature, excellency, and comfort of a truly broken and contrite spirit. So that what is here written is but a transcript out of his own heart: for God – who had much work for him to do – was still hewing and hammering him by his Word, and sometimes also by more than ordinary temptations and desertions.

Cokayn identified for the reader the reason and purpose of such a way of God's working in Bunyan's life:

The design, and also the issue thereof, through God's goodness, was the humbling and keeping of him low in his own eyes. The truth is, as himself sometimes acknowledged, he always needed the thorn in the flesh, and God in mercy sent it him, lest, under his extraordinary circumstances, he should be exalted above measure; which perhaps was the evil that did more easily beset him than any other.

But then as a true friend of Bunyan's, Cokayn issued a warning in Bunyan's own style:

O let none who peruse this book herd with that generation of hardened ones, but be a companion of all those that mourn in Zion and whose hearts are broken for their own, the church's, and the nation's provocations; who indeed, are the only likely ones that will stand in the gap to divert judgments.

Elizabeth Bunyan had found several unpublished manuscripts her husband had prepared for the printer. Following counsel, she published a newspaper advertisement of her willingness to print the manuscripts with the assistance of any who would be interested in seeing them published. After reading the advertisement, Bunyan's London friend Charles Doe visited Elizabeth in Bedford to view the manuscripts and arrange their publication.

In 1691, a folio of ten manuscripts under the title *The Struggler* was published by Charles Doe, who called himself "one of Mr. Bunyan's personal friends" and testified that "I have struggled to bring about this great good work." By his own testimony, this young comb-maker had only known Bunyan for two years; yet Doe's work on Bunyan's behalf is an invaluable source of information about the publication of Bunyan's works.

The Struggler was actually a catalog of the sixty works published and a list of thirty reasons why subscribers should invest in so worthy a cause as the printing of the works of the late John Bunyan. Doe included a short biography of John Bunyan with the apology that the brevity must be accounted to his brief acquaintance with Bunyan and Doe's own hurry to go to press. He confirmed to the readers, however, that "if any more comes to my memory, I intend to put it at the end of the index."

In 1698, Doe published *The Heavenly Footman*, written by Bunyan about 1668.

It is doubtful that even faithful Charles Doe could have envisioned the scope of Bunyan's influence. *The Struggler*, with its ten manuscripts, was financed in part by "about four hundred subscriptions" that proved to Doe "the great esteem our author's labours are in among Christian people." Mr. Doe could not have imagined in those days of 1691 London, that his own struggles would reap such benefits for Christians worldwide for centuries. *The Pilgrim's Progress* alone has never been out of publication since its original publication and now includes translations into more than two hundred languages. A multitude of volumes of notes and commentary have been written on the two parts of *The Pilgrim's Progress* and *The Holy War*. Countless sermons have been preached and lectures have been given on these allegories and their applications to the lives of Christians. Bunyan's writings have been quoted and studied as theological texts and literary texts. He has been quoted by Christians and those claiming no faith. The branches of Bunyan's tree have spread worldwide.

John Bunyan was indeed a man of his times. His own personal coming to Christ in salvation was fraught with turbulence of soul; but the life and times of his Bedford, at that time of his life, enjoyed the liberty of religious worship under the helm of the Nonconformists. During his walk of Christian sanctification, however, turbulence was in the world of England around him; and Nonconformists were no longer legal. Bunyan would spend his Christian life suffering the effects of monarchial religious disputes. Even when the threat of a Roman Catholic resurgence was at bay, the Established Church afforded Bunyan no relief. He had refused to be spiritually restricted by any other than the God of the Scriptures; and for this, he was held in contempt by both monarch and Established clergy.

Bunyan spent his adult life in the service of the King, often to the disturbance of the king and his men. But as his earthly life was drawing to a close, he may not have been aware of the success of the political negotiations to bring William of Orange and Mary to the English throne. In November 1688, William and his troops landed at Torbay. James II, left without allies, fled to France. Charles Doe wrote that shortly after John Bunyan was buried "our great gospel deliverance was begun by the Prince of Orange's landing, whom the Lord of his continued blessing hath since made our preserving king, William the Third." It was England's Glorious Revolution.

But Bunyan was already gone to his glorious homecoming. His life had been filled with the enduring riches of Christ. His sermons and his writings were his heart turned inside out. His tears were for his family and always for those who heard his Gospel preaching. He longed to know Christ in His fullness and to point others to such a blessed Savior.

The fires of persecution purge dross, but they also forge friendships and kindred spirits in things divine. Bunyan was never at a loss for such friendships, nor did he fail to recognize those gifts. He understood the necessity of Galatians 6:2: *Bear ye also one another's burdens, and so fulfill the law of Christ.* Such a poignant illustration of the love of brethren is found in *The Pilgrim's Progress*:

> *Christian cried, "Stay, stay, till I come to you;" but Faithful answered, "No, I am upon my life, and the avenger of blood is behind me."*
>
> *At this Christian was somewhat moved, and putting to all his strength, he quickly got up with Faithful, and did also overrun him; so the last was first. Then did Christian vaingloriously smile, because he had gotten the start of his brother: but not taking good heed to his feet, he suddenly stumbled and fell, and could not rise again until Faithful came up to help him.*

How those words of Sir John Kelynge echo through the corridors of time that Bunyan must follow his calling of tinkering and leave off preaching or be banished. What horror to think of the riches lost to the world if Bunyan had done just that! For Justice Sir John Kelynge's voice, speaking on behalf of the king, was silenced by the grave to speak no more except in the echoed reverberations against John Bunyan. But the voice of John Bunyan, preaching tinker of Bedford, continues to be heard. Would not Sir John and his fellow justices find their marvel at a preaching tinker to be far surpassed by the marvel that the voice they had hoped to silence would ring aloud in Bunyan's very words repeated in the Anglican Order of Service for the funeral of

H. M. Queen Elizabeth, the Queen Mother, on 9 April 2002.

Bunyan himself was surely speaking in the words of his own Mr. Standfast, who just as Bunyan had done, set things in order since the time had come for him to be away:

> *This river has been a terror to many; yea, the thoughts of it also have often frightened me; but now methinks I stand easy, my foot is fixed upon that on which the feet of the priests that bare the ark of the covenant stood, while Israel went over this Jordan. The waters indeed are to the palate bitter, and to the stomach cold: yet the thought of what I am going to, and of the conduct that waits for me on the other side, doth lie as a glowing coal at my heart. I see myself now at the end of my journey; my toilsome days are ended. I am going to see that head that was crowned with thorns, and that face that was spit upon for me. I have formerly lived by hear-say and faith; but now I go where I shall live by sight, and shall be with him in whose company I delight myself.* **I have loved to hear my Lord spoken of; and wherever I have seen the print of his shoe in the earth, there I have coveted to set my foot too.**

John Bunyan's Tomb

Endnotes

Introduction

[1] J. H. Merle D'Aubigne, D.D., *History of the Reformation of the Sixteenth Century, Volumes I to V* (Grand Rapids: Baker Book House, 1976), 384.

[2] Ibid., 193.

[3] Ernest W. Bacon, *John Bunyan: Pilgrim and Dreamer* (Grand Rapids: Baker Book House, 1984), 20.

Chapter 1

[4] Ibid., 9-11.

[5] Ibid., 10; Vera Brittain, *In the Steps of John Bunyan: An Excursion into Puritan England* (London: Rich & Cowan, 1950), 41, https://archive.org/details/instepsofjohnbun00brituoft.

[6] Vera Brittain, *In the Steps of John Bunyan: An Excursion into Puritan England,* 44.

[7] Ibid., 24.

Chapter 2

[8] Ernest W. Bacon, *John Bunyan: Pilgrim and Dreamer,* 42-43.

[9] Frank Mott Harrison, *John Bunyan: A Story of His Life* (Edinburgh: The Banner of Truth Trust, 1989), 12.

[10] Puritan Arthur Dent graduated from Christ's College, Cambridge in 1579. As a minister in the Established Church, he found himself in trouble with his bishop for some nonconformist behavior. He also signed a petition disagreeing with the statement that the Book of Common Prayer did not contain anything contrary to God's Word. Dent died in 1607. The original title of his book written in 1601 was *The plaine mans path-way to heauen: wherein euery man may clearly see, whether he shall be saued or damned: set forth dialogue wise, for the better understanding of the simple.*

[11] Puritan Lewis Bayly was a bishop in the Established Church whose book *The Practice of Piety* was translated into several languages, making it the most purchased reformed book of

the 1600s. The complete title was *The Practice of Piety, directing a Christian how to walk that he may please God.* Bayly died in 1631.

Chapter 3

[12] In *The Holy War*, Bunyan's name for the Holy Spirit of God was the Lord Chief Secretary.

[13] American Tract Society, ed., *The Pilgrim's Progress* (New York: D. Fanshaw, no date), 5.

[14] This word "burthen" is an archaic synonym for the word "burden."

Chapter 4

[15] Frank Mott Harrison, *John Bunyan: A Story of His Life,* 37.

[16] Vera Brittain, *In the Steps of John Bunyan: An Excursion into Puritan England,* 158.

[17] Frank Mott Harrison, *John Bunyan: A Story of His Life*, 71.

[18] Vera Brittain, *In the Steps of John Bunyan: An Excursion into Puritan England*, 176.

[19] Assizes were periodic court sessions for civil and criminal cases held in the seven circuits of England and Wales and conducted by travelling judges who set up court and called out juries in each of the assize towns.

[20] "Forlorn hope" is an interesting military term of Dutch origin meaning "lost band." Bunyan would have understood it to mean the first group of soldiers used to begin an attack in a siege. Their object was to secure a foothold by breaking through the defenses, but the hope of their own survival was very slim. Modern usage refers to an extremely difficult or even hopeless undertaking. Bunyan obviously saw himself as the first of many Christians who would suffer as the Clarendon Code became law. Since he understood this suffering as inevitable, he was concerned that he remained the committed, faithful example to those who would follow, just as the band of soldiers called the forlorn hope.

Chapter 5

[21] In Bunyan's own account, he refers to this man as Justice Keelin. In an 1873 memoir of Bunyan, the writer refers to this justice as Keeling and believed him to be the same man known as Chief-Justice Kelynge. Different spellings were common in those days.

[22] In January 1661, a group of Fifth Monarchy men, led by Thomas Venner, attempted a coup in London against King Charles II under the guise of religion.

[23] Ernest Bacon, *John Bunyan: Pilgrim and Dreamer*, 105.

Chapter 6

[24] Ibid., 91.

[25] These two laws were part of the notorious Clarendon Code. The Conventicle Act of 1664 outlawed religious meetings not of the Established Church with more than five people in attendance. As a result, many Nonconformist ministers had to leave their churches; but many of the members of their congregations also left and met with these ministers in secluded places in the country. The Five Mile Act of 1665 was even harsher. Aimed particularly at the Nonconformists, it forbid these ministers from preaching, teaching, living, or even coming within five miles of any city or town where they had previously preached or taught, unless they took an oath of allegiance to the Established Church.

[26] Vera Brittain, *In the Steps of John Bunyan: An Excursion into Puritan England,* 257.

[27] Ibid., 19, 294.

[28] Ibid., 19-22, 294-297.

Chapter 7

[29] Rev. Jeremiah Chaplin, ed., *The Riches of Bunyan Selected from His Works* (New York: American Tract Society, 1850), 481,
http://books.google.com/books/about/The_Riches_of_Bunya n.html?id=aUkQAAAAYAAJ.

[30] *The Pilgrim's Progress: From This World to That Which is to Come* (New Haven: John Babcock & Son, 1821), vii-viii.
[31] Frank Mott Harrison, *John Bunyan: A Story of His Life,* 176.

http://www.cowetaparticularbaptist.org

http://www.sermonaudio.com/source_detail.asp?sou rceid=cpbf